THE ST. MARYSTOWN SAGA ---

Dick Dornisch's St. Marystown Saga

Written and Illustrated

By

Richard J. Dornisch

Edited and Digitized

by

D. "Bucky" Lecker

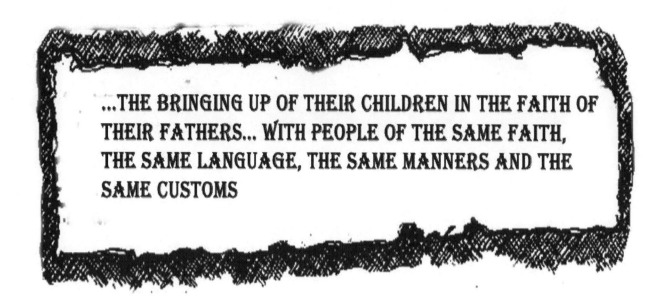

...THE BRINGING UP OF THEIR CHILDREN IN THE FAITH OF THEIR FATHERS... WITH PEOPLE OF THE SAME FAITH, THE SAME LANGUAGE, THE SAME MANNERS AND THE SAME CUSTOMS

Book design cover by Martin Dornisch

Introduction
by Richard "Dick" Dornisch

I suppose it could be said that the St. Marystown Saga began as an afterthought. Early in my career as a columnist for the Daily Press, I created a panel that would run every week for ten years. I called it, "The Way I see It." The format pictured five faces, usually St. Marys town folks, responding to a serious or facetious query. Nearly 2,500 local and nearby personalities appeared in the local paper during its decade-long run.

As the 50th anniversary of the Invasion of Fortress Europe neared, I began a second feature and called it, "From the Front." Here, I attempted to relive the final days of WWII with quips from the news as they had developed locally, nationally, and on an international level. I utilized slogans, newspaper/magazine articles, and stanzas from old wartime songs, both Allied and Axis.

This all made the column popular, and with "The Way I See It," Saturday's edition appeared to be the most anticipated daily of the week. Much of the WWII's attraction resulted from my using what, for the most part, were unpublished photos of St. Marys service men and women. Nearly 500 were depicted, bringing about one in every three folks who served to the pages of the Press fifty years after the fact. However, the war and its aftermath could only be utilized for so long. When it ended, it was clear that I needed to do something else.

I had often thought of creating a strip history of the community but was also conscious of the fact that it would be extremely demanding, both in the drawing requirements and because of the need for thousands of hours of reading microfilm, available histories, journals, diaries, etc. Still, I decided to give it a shot and on the last Saturday of August in 1995, the first panel appeared on the front page, predicated upon the following: "The St. Marystown Saga would appear weekly on the back page of the Saturday edition."

A few final words as to its success or failure: There were two aspects to the project that would hopefully make it different from the histories of St. Marys previously written. About the time that I had become associated with the local Historical Society, it had fallen into the hands of some young Turks, such as Ray Beimel, Ann Grosser, Don Fleming, Gary Kraus, Den McGeehan, and others who were no longer going to be satisfied with undocumented oral history and local folklore.

All at once the old stories were not what they had seemed. Even the lists of the original settlers and their reasons for creating the community were not what many had thought. Accounts of the original settlers and their reasons for braving a new colony were ambiguous and questionable, and I would hope to rely on facts or at least studied speculation in my storytelling.

Furthermore, in the past most histories were considered to be narrowly oriented. Available were the histories written by Schaut, Goetz, Lenze, and a host of others. Likewise, some of the more valued early documents had been lost to the town because of rivalries and inconsistencies in the earlier stories, and I hoped to avoid the personal and familiar aspects.

The second thing I wished to emphasize was a more holistic approach to the St. Mary tale that had previously been attempted. I did not wish to depict the Colony as being isolated or disconnected from the surrounding nation and world. My intention was to place the early history of little village within the context of world history, technological change – and everything in between – and wished to demonstrate the manner that

6

exterior events influenced the growth of and future of
St. Marystown.

Consequently, the reader will frequently encounter strips
that seem not to pertain to St. Marys at all - except by
the nature of their influence on society and the rest of
the world.

-Dick Dornisch

8

Forward

In the Introduction to the Saga, Dick Dornisch wrote:

"I had often thought of creating a strip history of the community but was also conscious of the fact that it would be extremely demanding…"

Likewise, an effort to extract Dick's research, text, and drawings from his personal collection of 380-plus strips would also prove to be a monumental task for which it might have been difficult set aside enough time.

Then, usher in a PANDEMIC which would free me from some of my work duties for several months.

Thus, *Dick Dornisch's St. Marystown Saga* came to be.

The digitization process required that I erase the text from the drawings, remove any background, alter the threshold, copy and paint the canvas black. Then, I added a mask, cropped, rotated, flipped, adjusted, inverted, pasted, scaled, proofread, while attending to any missing aspect.

Thereafter, it was necessary to type the handwritten textual content.

Because the work was originally a weekly publication and produced in comic strip form, the transition to standard print in book form required substantial editing.

So, I redrew, skewed, flipped, and stretched many drawings. I also added three images which I copied from the internet, all of which were gratefully extracted from the Public Domain.

Granted, when Dick was writing the Saga, the internet was a rather new phenomenon to which he had limited access.

I'll agree that some images are sharp, while others are soft. Given that Dick's original copies were of a varying degree of detail, there was no other option than to vary many of the procedures by which the pen and inks would be digitized.

Quite often, it seemed necessary to capture the emotion of an image after having digitized it, which necessitated an original approach; and, as I progressed through the project, my technological competencies improved.

While capturing the images, I would frequently ask myself:

Does the digitization communicate the artistic emotion?

Can I improve anything?

How much do I need to draw to complete the areas interrupted by handwritten text?

When comparing the present rendition to the original, one will recognize that many images have been horizontally flipped. In this regard, I'll confess to spinning the pictures around and around until I was convinced that the perspective communicated the artist's intention for the drawing, and the alteration served a necessary juxtaposition regarding the text.

I also attempted to carefully utilize space, often spreading paragraphs to many lines.

In the words of one of my former educational supervisors "Less is more."

Regarding the level of the "threshold," my technique was to revisit the original and then review the digitized version. When the emotions depicted on the subject's faces were conveyed in the scan, I recognized such was the limit of the transition.

The order of the Saga titles might not be 100% accurate, but it is close enough. I don't believe any (or many) are missing.

The aforesaid process was that of constant revision, and the effort might just have neglected various artistic intentions in exchange for completion.

Sincerely,

D. Bucky Lecker

Table of Contents

After centuries of little population growth, Europe underwent an unexplained explosion of human births.

Civil and social unrest were rampant but following the defeat of Napoleon, the continent would enjoy almost a century without a major war.

It was the eve of the Industrial Revolution and science, philosophy, and the arts were challenging religious & cultural traditions.

In America, the far west was the domain of the trapper and mountain man.

The Gold Rush was still a decade away and with it the settling of the West.

The United States was on the brink of an unpopular war with Mexico, which can be thought to have been the beginning of the Civil War. Across the ocean, France, Spain, Russia, and England were considered to be threats to the young nation.

John Tyler was the President of the United States and the first Vice President to assume office after of the death of a chief executive. He was very much a man without a Party who vetoed nearly every bill sent to his office and became the first president to be threatened with impeachment.

Long having been regarded as lack-luster, some historians consider him to have been a national leader of great integrity and personal courage.

During Tyler's first term, wagon trains began to head west, and a small band of German Catholic merchants and farmers established a tiny settlement in Central PA that would become **St. Marys, Pennsylvania.**

PENNSYLVANIA BACKGROUND:

Founded in 1681 by **William Penn**, an English Quaker upstart, and granted by the Crown for debts owed to his father, Penn's Wood's (Pennsylvania, as named by Parliament) became a haven for religious and political freethinkers during the French and Indian wars.

William Penn was a friend of the Native American, and they shared a mutual respect, honoring their treaties. The same was not true of the great Quaker's heirs who offered **bounties on** Indians, dead or alive.

The French and English claimed much of the same land in western PA, which was a cause of the French and Indian wars.

The French established Fort Lee Boeuf in present day Waterford in Erie County.

Pennsylvania was also the scene of military activity in the west, a hot bed of sedition, and the locale of the 1st American revolt against the government.

We now call this uprising *"THE WHISKEY REBELLION."*

In 1749, a Captain Celoron journeyed to the Warren area where it is said that he buried a lead plate where Allegheny and Conewango meet, claiming the land for France.

It has never been found.

Baltimore in 1838 was one of the busiest places in North America.

It was close enough to Washington and Philadelphia to be a hive of political and commercial activity and intrigue. Many Europeans disembarked there seeking employment.

That same year **Jacob Schaut**, 28 years old, arrived in New York from Bavaria, the kingdom Napoleon invented in 1805.

Schaut did not stay in New York but went to Baltimore both seeking work and attempting to connect to fellow countrymen.

Already by 1830, the sons of the men who made the Revolution and adopted the lofty words of the Declaration of Independence and Constitution were shouting "America for Americans."

In Pennsylvania and Maryland, Schaut encountered growing resentment, first as a "furriner" but especially as a "Papist" and probable foreign agent as Catholics were said to have been.

[We'll leave Jacob Schaut in Baltimore working odd jobs as a handyman and journeyman carpenter.]

27

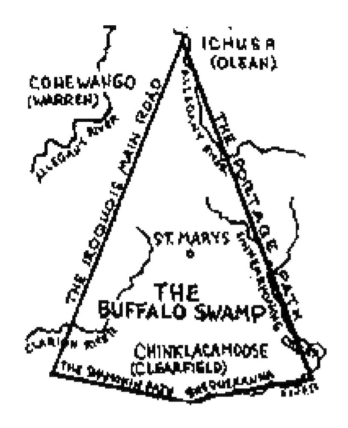

In the early history of the state, most of northern Pennsylvania from the Allegheny to the east branch of the Susquehanna consisted of a vast unpopulated wilderness.

A few Indian trails passed through the area, but Native Americans rarely hunted in the "Great Swamp" or "Buffalo Swamp" to the west, referring to these places as "Shades of Death."

The isosceles triangle they called the "Buffalo Swamp" contained much of much of present-day Elk, Cameron, McKean, Jefferson, and Clearfield counties.

Four Native American roads lied on the parameters of the Buffalo Swamp. On the west side was the main road of the Iroquois - or Catawba trail - which ran south all the way to Tennessee.

On the east side, the Portage Path spanned north from central Pennsylvania through present day Emporium to Ichsua (Olean).

To the south, the triangle was bounded by the Vanango-Chinklamoose and Shamokin paths.
Old maps do not show a hunting trail inside this triangle.

In 1840, BALTIMORE, where St. Marys can be said to have begun, was in a bustling seaport-with one of the finest harbors in the world.

It was a sailor and Fisherman's town and a landing place for many European immigrants.

It was also the largest Catholic center in the new nation and the location of the first Catholic Bishopric.

During the Revolution, the capital was moved to Baltimore for three months when the British threatened Philadelphia.

CECIL CALVERT was the second of three Lord Baltimore's associated with the city. He founded the colony of Maryland and drafted laws granting religious freedom to the people.

When the Maryland Assembly passed these freedom laws in 1649, the city became the first enclave of religious freedom in the colonies.

CHARLES CARROL of Carrollton lived to be the last surviving signature of the Declaration of Independence (737-1832).

This prominent Marylander and member of the Continental Congress was also the only Catholic to sign the Document.

The brothers, Daniel, who signed the Articles of Confederation, and John, the first Roman Catholic Bishop of America, were great patriots like their cousin, Charles.

When Reverend John Carrol, the Bishop of Baltimore, let it be known that he opposed churches of ethnic or national character, it is likely that in doing so he created the conditions resulting in the formation of the St. Marystown Colony.

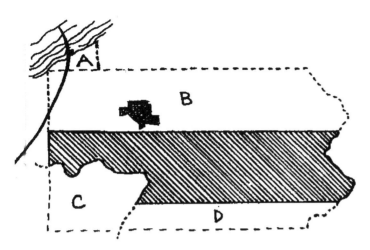

Besides much of western Pennsylvania's ownership having been disputed by the French and English during its early history, it was also claimed by New York (A), Connecticut (B), Virginia (C), and Maryland (D).

Although we don't often think of it, the state also boarders a foreign nation.

By the end of the 18th century, two counties made up most of western & north central Pennsylvania, (I) Allegheny and (II)

Northumberland. In much of this vast and unsettled territory, the population was less than three persons per square mile.

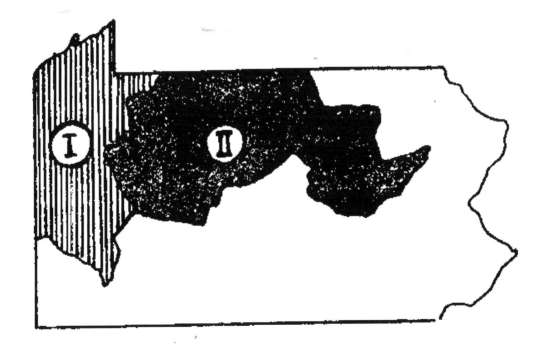

It is unlikely that anyone will ever know who the first Europeans to enter Elk Country were, but tradition suggests that the Bennetts came up the Susquehanna into what is present day Caledonia in 1780. They did not stay, but they gave their names to Bennett's Valley.

In 1798 a **General Wade**, his family, and a man named **Slade** – who was probably the General's aide or Lieutenant - came into Elk County via the little Toby.

Slade would later court and marry a squaw who became known as the "Maid of Blue Rock" (Spring Creek).

Amos David, who settled in Fox Township in 1810, is believed to have been the first permanent settler in Elk County.

Enter the man who can be thought of as the most important and interesting figure in St. Marys history:

His name is **Father Alexander Cvitkowitz C.S.S.R. (1806-1863).**

He was neither German nor Benedictine, but rather, a young Hungarian nobleman and member of the congregation of the Holy Redeemer (Redemptorists).

In 1840, when Joseph Schaut arrived in Baltimore, his order had been well established. The Redemptorists were founded by St. Alphonsus in Italy in 1732.

In the 19th century, the Catholic Sect was attracting Poles, Bohemians and Austrians from the Noble houses of Eastern and Central Europe.

These were the same men who in an earlier time would have been protecting Europe from the Ottomans in the armies of Hunyadi Janos and King Sobieski.

Cvitkowitz was ordained in 1830, and for a couple of years the energetic priest was assigned to Austria.

He later became prior of a boy's school in the low countries and in 1836 established the redemptorists in Witten. In 1840, he was appointed rector of the Order's House in Vienna.

By most accounts, Father Alexander answered the call for priests to administer to the many German Catholics living without clergy in America.

A romantic version of the story has it that the Redemptorists, like the rest of European society, were captivated by the noble American savage portrayed in the novels of James Fenimore Cooper, Chateaubriand and wished to work among them. Given the adventurous heritage of these men, it seems possible that the first five Redemptorists sailed for American before end of 1840.

Because of Willian Penn's socio-religious-radical-liberalism and the privacy of the great unpopulated Pennsylvania wilderness, a proliferation of experimental settlements sprung up in the early 1800s.

Almost all of them had "self-destruct" built into their concepts and charters.

Aelesia was established for Marie Antionette (who never visited the place) and other aristocratic refugees of the French Revolution. Ephrata Cloister and Harmony settlements were communities of celibates and depended on the world ending to be successful.

Among some of the other known Pennsylvania colonies included the Moravian towns of Nazareth, Bethlehem, and Celestia, which sued to secede and was eventually deeded to God (who neglected to pay his taxes).

The Norwegian violinist, Ole Bull, formed a famous "Lost Colony" in the wilds of Potter County, and a group of German Catholics created a tiny Bavarian Catholic commune in the depths of the Buffalo swamp and called it, **MARIENSTADT**.

Belgium and Holland in the 1800s were fertile grounds for evolving theological and social concepts, just as they are at this writing.

The young Father Alexander Cvitkowitz, C.SS.R., would most certainly have been exposed to these theories during his tenure in the low countries.

Before his first year ended in America, he too would have an opportunity to form a new religious commune.

A NOTE FROM THE STORYTELLER...

To retell a story such as the founding of St. Marys, it is necessary to
use old oral tradition and the work of the earlier local historians, adding new
information and studied speculation.

This work is an interpretation, no more likely to be correct or complete than any
previous or future version.

-Dick Dornisch

The scarcity of priests in the mid-1800s states caused many of the cloth to be held hostage by the Catholic populations in American towns and cities.

Within weeks after Father Alexander's arrival from Europe, he was appointed Prior of the Church of the Holy Redeemer in Baltimore.

The Redemptorists were not destined to work with Native Americans.

When and under what conditions Schaut and Father Alexander met might never be known, but Schaut was gilding and doing minor repairs in Baltimore churches in mid-1841.

Given the chronology of events, the first proposal for a new settlement was made soon after the meeting.

Investigation by St. Marys' Historians does not find a Church of the Holy Redeemer in Baltimore in 1840 where it was said that Schaut and Alexander met.

There was, however, a run-down St. Alphonsus Church under the auspices of the redemptorists at the time. (Hence the mistaken name).

The congregation was made up of less than well-to-do Bavarians and Alsatians.

St. Alphonsus also seems to have sprung from the Church of St. John Evangelist, built as a strictly German establishment in opposition to Bishop Carroll's directions.

In response to the schism, Carroll enlisted a militia to prevent services, and an armed confrontation took place between soldiers and parishioners.

It is important to remember that most of the early settlers were from St. John's Parish.

The firebrand pastor disappeared after the incident, some say going West and joining many other intriguing figures who disappeared into the mists of history after a radical start.

Enter the enigmatic figure of **Mattius Benzinger** (1800-1874), believed by some early historians to have been the father of the colony.

Recent investigations indicate that he was probably as much con artist as patron. He was called "Colonel" most of his life and may have earned that rank in the Maryland Militia.

Benzinger was born to a family of minor German nobility in Forchheim, Baden, Germany.

He arrived in the states as a young man but how he acquired his considerable wealth is not known.

Some indications are that he was involved with government contract work in Baltimore and Washington.

"Colonel" Benzinger, who seems to have been a busy gentleman, fathered eight children with his first wife who died before 1850. He then married a much younger lady and begot twelve more kids.

There is evidence suggesting that Benzinger was a stockholder in the Fox Land Company of Boston. This is the same company which owned the land purchased to establish the colony of St. Marys.

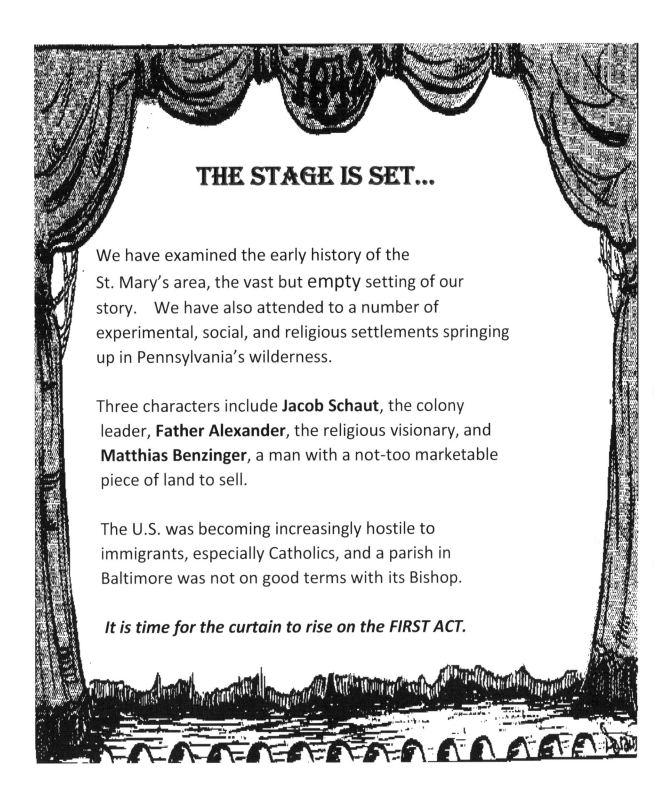

THE STAGE IS SET...

We have examined the early history of the
St. Mary's area, the vast but empty setting of our
story.   We have also attended to a number of
experimental, social, and religious settlements springing
up in Pennsylvania's wilderness.

Three characters include **Jacob Schaut**, the colony
leader, **Father Alexander**, the religious visionary, and
Matthias Benzinger, a man with a not-too marketable
piece of land to sell.

The U.S. was becoming increasingly hostile to
immigrants, especially Catholics, and a parish in
Baltimore was not on good terms with its Bishop.

It is time for the curtain to rise on the FIRST ACT.

We are not likely to ever discover exactly what Czvikovicz and Schaut discussed in their early talks, but the idea for a colony seems to have been the obvious topic

Were Schaut and Father Alexander to have been the originators of the colony idea, the German Catholic Brotherhood of Baltimore and Philadelphia were the stepfathers.

The group formed in response to the ever more strident political moves against Catholic immigrants.

There are conflicting dates and puzzling chronologies in the pre-colony history, but on and unknown date in 1840, a series of meetings took place in Philadelphia between representatives for the colony and officials from Baltimore to discuss the founding of a Catholic enclave for Germans in the Wilds of PA.

Philadelphia and Baltimore are about 100 miles apart by primitive railway or stagecoach, and much farther by sailing vessels.

That such meetings could have taken place is rather puzzling.

At one of the first of their gatherings, they decided that a party should be sent into North Central Pennsylvania to seek possible colony sites.

But, before following the three explorers, **Albert**, **Reimel,** and **Derleth** into the heart of the Buffalo Swamp, it will be necessary to meet a fourth player, **Mr. Ignatius Garner**.

If any community was ever blessed with a man for all seasons, it was early St. Marys in the person of **Ignatius Garner**.

Czvikovicz and Schaut have been called the visionaries, and Garner is thought of as the pragmatist.

The cleric and journeyman's ideas were in many ways Utopian, but Garner, no less a visionary, had both good ideas which worked and the energy to see them through.

Garner arrived in the States from Alsace-Lorrain with his parents in 1832. Fluent in English, French and German, he served as a teacher in Cincinnati and in Jasper, Ill, for eight years. In 1840 he returned to Philadelphia and worked as an organist and choir master.

Philadelphia is thought to be where he made the acquaintances of Schaut and Father Alexander.

Sometime around 1840, according to Garner's obituary, he rescued two young ladies from drowning, resulting in an illness that cost him some hearing loss.

According to historian Charles Schaut, Garner met the other principals in this story very early, but no written records exist to support the contention. What is known is that by 1845, his importance to St. Marys can hardly be exaggerated.

His sister Magdalena would marry Jacob Schaut, and he would marry Julia Weis, the daughter of George Weis, an early settler and the village's 1st merchant.

The Schaut, Garner, and Weis family might just be the most important family's in St. Marys' history.

Most with those names in St. Marys are descendants of these essential families.

Who were the three men who made the initial trek into the North Central Pennsylvania Wilderness for the German Catholic Brotherhood?

Were they members of the Brotherhood? Were they committed to the idea of a colony? Were they accomplished woodsmen or young adventurers?

It is unlikely that we will ever know, but we do have reason to believe that none of them ever returned as permanent settlers to the area whose purchase they recommended.

In the earliest days of the Commonwealth, William Penn envisioned a canal system to serve as a means of moving people and products across the state.

The map below depicts the central and eastern systems, both ending in Milesburg.

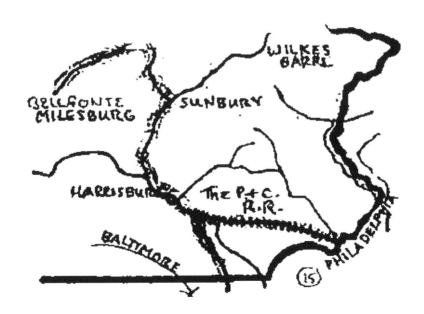

The canal systems were far removed from the Buffalo Swamp or that territory termed, "Shippen."

Today we call the area Elk, Potter, McKean, and Cameron counties.

Where the canal ended, a lonely trail called the Milesburg-Smethport Turnpike meandered through a dark, dense forest.

Hardy souls can still hike 2/5ths or so of the original route, from the present-day Caledonia Pike, starting in Karthus. Along the way, several toll houses once stood. Most of these had been grants given to Revolutionary War veterans.

Tradition has it that Albert, Reimel and Derleth traveled to the present-day Potter County area to investigate properties to serve as land for the new settlement.

However, the discovery that Benzinger was a partner in the Fox Land Company raises the suspicion that the choice was made before the men ever left Philadelphia.

We do know that they never travelled past Centerville.

Although old stories say the three men departed in March and returned in May, documentation does not seem to exist.

A meeting, which might have been the first of many, was held on June 2nd.

The three men who had gone out to find suitable land for a settlement had agreed to purchase 30,000 acres from the Fox Land Company at 75 cents an acre.

An impractical, utopian, octagon shaped city plan was possibly laid out by the redemptorists the summer before anyone had ever seen the terrain.

Somehow, during the summer in 1842 in the cities of Baltimore and Philadelphia, a group of people assembled who were willing to risk their futures and life savings on a colony in an unmapped wilderness.

At this point in the story, many questions arise: Who was the leader of the first group(s)? Why were they recruited, and how was the planning accomplished between the two cities?

But, was there even a plan? And, why would such an undertaking be launched in October? To those familiar with the weather in north central Pennsylvania, such an endeavor on borders on insanity.

And who were these folks?

Were they malcontents, adventurers, people afraid of growing urban anti-Catholic feeling, or people at loggerheads with their own Bishop?

We may never know, but by late October 13 family units had been recruited, consisting of 12 husbands and wives with an unrecorded number of children and Jacob Schaut, the only unmarried adult with the first group.

Fr. Alexander Czvikowicz -- Probably originated the idea. Religious & Civic Leader
Benzinger, Col. Matiah -- Land owner, speculator, or colony benefactor.
Eshbach, Joseph, Von Schroeder, Baron, Cartuyvals, Fr. "Louie" C.S.S.R, were all associates of
Benzinger in the St. Marystown Colony gamble.

The explorers and Land purchasers:
Albert, John
Derleth, Michael
Reimal, Nicholas

* Was Albert - as a result of having been a member of the original group and the Executive Committee of the German Catholic Brotherhood - the real leader of the first group of settlers?

WE do know that by 1845 he was again residing in Philadelphia.

Executive Committee of the German Catholic Brotherhood of Phila & Balt.
Albert, John
Derleth, Michael
Reimel, Nicholas
Stockman, Adolph
Kernhaas, John, Sec.
Brechtenwald, Peter
Shad, John
Schweitzer, Mathias

(-) - Indicates the known number in a family.

Although the idea for the Colony appears to have come from Baltimore, Philidelpha seems to have provided early leadership.

The first Philadelphia settlers:
Albert, John
Stockman, Adolph (5)
Evers (Avis etc.) Anthony
Hill, Nicholas
Keller, George (4)
Kock, Herman
Vornbaum, Julius (3)
Walker, John
Wellendorf, Nicholas

The First Baltimore Settlers

Adelberger, John (4)
Geyer, Bartholomeus (2)
Heubel, Benedict (6)
Schaut, Jacob
Scharlitzky, Andres (2)

- These families do not seem to have stayed in the Colony

Probably the entire Baltimore group were all members of the troubled old St. Alphonsus Parish

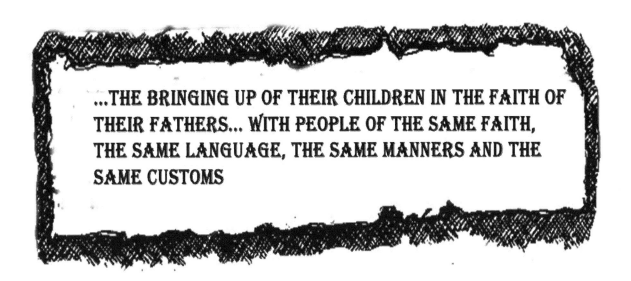

...THE BRINGING UP OF THEIR CHILDREN IN THE FAITH OF THEIR FATHERS... WITH PEOPLE OF THE SAME FAITH, THE SAME LANGUAGE, THE SAME MANNERS AND THE SAME CUSTOMS

Sometime during 1892, while the first settlers were being assembled, a charter to direct the colony was written. It was called the "Articles of the German Catholic Brotherhood."

It seems likely that the people who wrote the document were among the first settlers.

As the above wording from the Articles of the German Catholic Brotherhood shows, there was a definite stated intention to unite a colony not simply to German speakers, but German Catholic Bavarians.

Such was exactly the sort of fatal flaw that spelled doom for so many other ethnic-religious colonies in Pennsylvania.

Fortunately, Catholicism and Bavarian pragmatism did not lend itself willingly to bigotry.

It seems unlikely that father Czvikovicz or the Redemptorists had anything to do with the charter.

The order drew heavily on the Slavic countries and North Italy for its priests, and Czvikovicz himself was a Hungarian. Old maps also show that he planned from the beginning to establish a sister colony of Flemish Glass blowers in present day Glen Hazel.

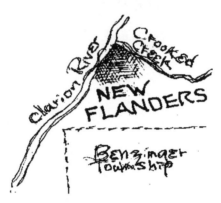

It is even more interesting to note that **Anthony Evers** of the Philadelphia group was Prussian, not Bavarian, while **Andres** and **Ann Maria Scharlitzky**, who replaced **Zinklemans** on the Baltimore list were most likely not even German.

If the charter ever had any influence on the colony, it couldn't have been much, for the group seems not to have taken it seriously.

The Philadelphia group consisting of nine married couples and their children were ready to leave the city around November 1st, 1842. Four additional family units plus Jacob Schaut would leave Baltimore about the same time but because of the extra distance, they would remain a few days behind.

Many of the treks into the Shippen territory carried on through the state canal system.

We may assume that like the roads in the Hinterlands, it too was a primitive affair in North Central Pennsylvania.

OF CANALS & CANAL BOATERS

Some romanticize the canals to this day, not unlike the lore surrounding steam locomotives and tall ships.

The most famous of the canals, the Erie (1825), connected the Great Lakes to the Atlantic Ocean via the Hudson River at Troy, NY.

Many canal and history buffs visit this old waterway every year.

Two old folk songs immortalize the canal days. They are both entitled, "The Erie Canal."

I had a mule her name was Sal
Fifteen miles on the Erie Canal
She's a good old worker and a good old pal...

And...

We were forty miles from Albany
Forget it, I never shall
What a terrible storm we had that night On the Erie, the Erie Canal...

60

Milesburg was a small riverside Village, situated a few miles N.W. from Bellefonte where the canal system ended.

Ahead lay 70 plus miles on the desolate and lonely Milesburg-Smethport Turnpike.

It's likely that it would have been necessary to hire wagons in Milesburg to transport babies and tools while the others walked.

61

No records exist to tell us that the settlers took their livestock with them, but it's quite likely that the family dogs and cats were not left behind.

In May 1982, seven St. Marys teenage boys were dropped off at Milesburg. From there they hiked to Karthus, Caledonia, Irishtown and across the hills to St. Marys. Closely following the route of the early settlers, they were three days and two nights on the 73-mile hike.

This was likely the first time the trek was made in over 100 years, and it rained all three days.

The group of boys included **Joel, Claude** and **Dan Dornisch, Sam Glatt, Vincent Munoz, Ray Rupprecht** and **Tim Hooper.**

The turnpike was the brainchild of **James Gillis** in 1823.

Gilles was an agent for **Jacob Ridgway** of Philadelphia, who with other agents who were interested in opening the North-Central wilderness, petitioned the commonwealth to form a company to build a toll road from Bald Eagle Creek, near Bellefonte and close to Geographical center of the state to the village of Smethport in McKean County.

Much of the Pike followed earlier trails and approximate five-mile sections were granted to toll collectors who kept the trail open. It was 120 miles in length. Some accounts have wolves and panthers frightening the travelers as they passed.

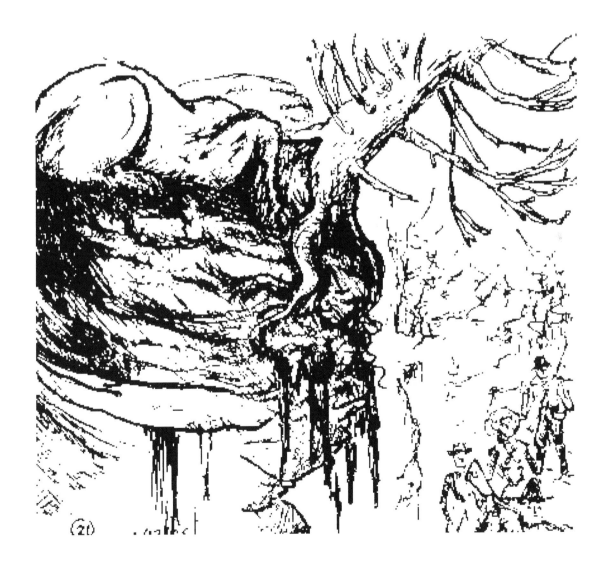

The settlements and the solitary cabins along the pike Northwest from Milesburg must have been few and far between from what we know of the population of the area in 1840.

It is likely that the settlers met few people before they reached the river village of Caledonia. Cooking and eating had to have been accomplished with little or no shelter along the way.

The St. Marys colony was much different that most Eastern U.S. towns, which seemingly evolved as ports, forts, river trading posts, crossroads, and markets.

CALEDONIA was the largest and most successful village in the area at the time, having begun as a fur trader's village and later a river lumber town.

It was the site of Elk County's first post office, sawmill, and courtroom.

Earlier in the year when Albert Derleth and Riemel were searching for land, they stayed John Green's establishment in Centreville. The first settlers would leave Green's inn and hack a trail through three miles of dense forest into the area that is present day St. Marys.

John Green (1799-1883) was a Quaker who came to Fox Township with his parents in 1817 and cleared a two-hundred-acre tract.

John's father was the first post-master in Centerville and later John would also hold the position.

He was a farmer and tavern/inn keeper who ran a toll station on the turnpike.

Journals of the trip do not exist, but certainly no one, notwithstanding people with little pioneering experience, could carry enough victuals to sustain a family through a Pennsylvania Wilds' winter.

Cracked wheat flour, corn meal, salt, dried apples, and root vegetables were likely purchased from Green and others when the settlers arrived in Centreville.

After getting the women and the children settled into the barn and outbuildings at Green's, the men proceeded a mile north to the tiny hamlet of Irishtown. From there they made their way through the dense, unbroken forest to the shadowed banks of the Elk Creek.

In late November 1842, they would begin to construct the crude Shelters where they and their families would endure the first winter.

Snow, wind, cold, and freezing rain are not uncommon in November, and a lack of woodland expertise is evident from records of the colony's men having been lost while traveling the trail between Green's farm and the cabins.

Some questions: Could their quarters have been called "cabins"?

Granted, the men would have had axes and hammers, but what of pit saws and broad axes?

Would they even had been able to use them?

How could the cabins have been built in November and occupied in January?

It has been said that the forest was so dense that trees had to be felled in creek beds or in lightening blasted areas to stop the surrounding trees from interfering with their fall.

Information about the actual construction and appearance of the first cabins is the result of studied speculation, much done by the work Paul and Bill Krellner.

The number of cabins needed was at least 13, and the number of men available were no more than 20. With four weeks of building time in November, and little time to dry logs or cut stone, the cabins would have to had been small and crudely constructed.

They were built from small logs, with few or no windows. A smokey (and dangerous) mud, stick and stone hearth provided a cooking fire and small amount of heat. Roofs were probably both peaked and made of logs, sod, and split boards.

The floors were bare earth. It is very unlikely that any sawed lumber was available at the time.

A few days after the men from Philadelphia left to begin building the first shelters at the colony site, the Baltimore group arrived at the Green Farm and tavern in Centreville.

Meanwhile in what would become the Saint Marystown settlement, work on the cabins continued daily from the first light until darkness.

At the end of a week of work, the men would hike back to Green's farm over a blazed trail to spend the weekend with their families.

On Monday they would return to their labors at the colony site.

With no records having been kept during this early period, accounts seem both contradictory and chronologically impossible, but it is likely that during the construction of the cabins, an intinerant Catholic priest visited the settlers briefly before moving on to Irishtown.

DECEMBER 8th, 1842, THE FEAST OF THE IMMACULATE CONCEPTION

WE HAVE NOW GOTTEN THE FIRST SETTLERS INTO THE AREA THAT WILL BECOME ST. MARYS...

When the 50 Year Jubilee commemorating the founding of the community was celebrated in 1892, many of the original settlers were still around to tell their tales.

But there are many unresolved questions:

What of the new list of the original settlers based on recent research?

Why, if the traditional list is wrong, didn't the surviving first settlers correct it during the Jubilee in 1892?????

What should we make of Rev. Alfred Watson's account of a priest celebrating mass in the two-story house of John Walker in mid-October 1842? That is about two weeks before the first group arrived in Centreville, Walker among them, told of a baby girl having been baptized at the settlement by an itinerant Father Predergast, Nov. 20, 1842. This doesn't seem likely, though.

Perhaps it could have occurred at the John Green farm by a priest making a call to Irishtown.

Now, another questions arise:

The Godmother is said to have been Maria Eva Lenz. Lenz is a name that does not appear on any first settler listing, and it is doubtful that anyone not of their group would be involved.

Many other questions and contradictions will be pointed out as our story continues, but as it unfolds, we might discover numerous more questions as history is never neat and finished but is subjective and sometimes even revisionist.

During the re-telling of the St. Marys story, criticisms and new and omitted material are solicited.

The settlers did survive their first winter in the colony, but no one will ever know just how they did it.

Imagine were one to challenge the winter cold in a smokey one or two room cabin on an earthen floor, which was same temperature as the outside air, while attending to the needs of several children and perhaps an infant.

Since there would have been little or no time to cut and dry firewood, every available hand was undoubtedly engaged in gathering fuel during every free moment.

Replenishing food supplies would have been constant and of the highest priority, and victuals must have been in short supply.

Water for cooking and a minimal degree of personal cleanliness would have required endless toil.

Candles and lamp oil would also have been a constant need.

The settlers would have had to rent or hire teams to make winter trips to established settlements for necessities.

After what must have seemed an eternity, March would at last arrive.

"If winter comes,
Can Spring be behind?"

-Percy Bysshe Shelley

With the arrival of spring came the departure of some of the original settlers.

Winter had been severe, and few of the settlers possessed the resources to return East.

But for those with little money, one winter in the Buffalo Swamp seemed quite enough.

Work on more substantial dwellings must have started as soon as the warm weather broke.

Also, wherever a patch had cleared, early planting would have gotten underway.

Additional arrivals would make their way to the colony with the return of warmer weather.

Among the newcomers were John Gerard, Nick Rittenwald, Joseph Dill, Charles Herbstritt, and Martin Herbstritt.

Many ethnic/religious oriented colonies established in late 19th century PA were in fact communes of a sort.

Likewise, much a of commune participant's possessions, especially food stores, were at least in theory communal property.

Prior to the overthrow of the Russian Romanovs, social communes were idealized and respected as a legitimate form of government.

Early Christian groups also practiced socialism and common ownership of material possessions.

As many other communal occupants had learned before, a few people couldn't work, and some people wouldn't work. Many were talented, while others were disasters.

Intentional communities in Pennsylvania settlements learned the same lessons in the mid-1800s, and the children of the 1960s experienced the same results all over again.

THE YOUNG MAN WHO WOULDN'T HOE CORN

I'll sing you a song, and it's not very long
'Bout a young man who wouldn't hoe his corn.
The reason why I cannot tell,
For that young man was always well.

He went down to his neighbor's door,
Where he had been many times before':
Pretty miss, pretty miss, will you marry me?
Pretty miss, pretty miss, what do you say?

Well, here you are a-waitin' to be wed,
And you cannot even make your own corn bread.
Single I be, and single I remain.
A lazy man I won't maintain.

...It was difficult to survive on the frontier without a spouse.

In 1843, the tiny colony was experiencing dark days with desertions and dissentions over work-sharing.

They also did not have a priest to regularly care for their spiritual needs.

Jacob Schaut, who was an old acquaintance of Father Alexander, was asked to travel to Baltimore and seek advice from a priest.

Schaut would become something of a traveling advocate for the colony in the early years, journeying to Bavaria to recruit new settlers and solicit financial support.

Czvikowicz arranged to have a missionary Redemptorist, Father Saenderl C.S.S.R., go to the Shippen Territory, which greatly helped the morale of the struggling colony.

Late in 1843, Father Alexander traveled from Baltimore to St. Marystown to evaluate his struggling brainchild in the heart of the wilderness of the PA Wilds.

He remained in the colony long enough make a few maps and recognize that the community was in danger of failing.

Czvikowicz then went back to Baltimore late in 1843, convinced that were the colony was going to survive, the financial burdens of the new settlers would have to be relieved and new terms adopted.

In Baltimore Czvikowicz looked for someone to assume the colony's financial burden. Expressing an early interest in the venture was Mattius Benzinger.

Benzinger and Eschbach had long been regarded as the saviors of the colony. Perhaps they were, but we would be remiss to ignore some other facts.

Benzinger was already a partner in the land company which owned the territory prior to the German Catholic Brotherhood's purchase of it, and the land was practically valueless with its lack of trails, and vast impenetrable forests.

Although Derleth, Reimek, and Albert traveled many hundreds of miles, when they reached Centreville, they purchased 30,000 acres of land, having neither seen nor set foot on it.

One might ponder the facts of the matter and conclude that after a group of settlers had committed their futures and fortunes to the venture and were, thereafter, fully engaged in clearing the land and cutting trails, the shadowy Col. Benzinger, and his even more shadowy partner, Eschbach, moved to re-acquire the property.

Clearly, suspicions would arise.

When Czvikowicz returned to Baltimore seeking investors to relieve the debt-ridden colony, Benzinger and his partner, Eschbach, were quick to show interest.

Benzinger then traveled to the colony, closed the deal with his partners in the Fox Land Co. and redistributed the land.

Each family unit which stayed was allotted a 100 x 200 square foot town lot and a 20-acre farm lot.

85

Among the earliest and most important personalities to arrive in the struggling colony in 1843 was Dame Dorthea Wolfram, a mid-wife hired by the Brotherhood in Baltimore.

Little is known of her activities, but she was the first professional medical practitioner to live in Sancta Marienstadt.

She arrived with her husband who farmed with his two teen-aged children. Her contract stated that the colony's needs were to come before any other consideration.

In 1864, her duties were taken over by a Madam Ringwald.

The first mass in the colony was likely celebrated in 1843 by the traveling missionary, Father Borgess, on the second floor of the newly erected John Walker home.

In May, Father Saenderl, who had been sent to the colony by Rev. Alexander Czvikowicz C.S.S.R., baptized Jacob Leitz, Catherine Keller, Philomena Wacker, and Margaret Reitenwald.

Among the names, only Keller is to be found in the list of the first settlers, which seems to indicate that when some of the first were returning to Baltimore and Philadelphia, other small groups were continuously arriving.

A collection of business associates and cronies of Col. Benzinger's who became associated with him in the St. Marystown venture included:

John Eschbach, (1798-1881) who was born in Baden, Germany and married an American woman from Washington D.C.   His wife seems to have had political or government connections.

It is thought that through his wife's influence, Eschbach acquired government contracts in the Washington/Baltimore area.

His considerable assets would have been attractive to the Colonel.

Of the Benzinger bunch, John Eschbach appears to have been the only one not to have visited his Elk County investment.

Father Jean Louis Cartuyvels (1811-8171) was born in St. Truden, Belgium in 1811 and is another one of the mysterious personalities with whom Benzinger allied.

Ordained a Redemptorist, he was dispensed of his vows in St. Marys in 1845. Consequently, he served at one time or another in numerous places as a Parish Secular, and in 1849 partnered with Benzinger and Eschbach.

Some argue that Cartuyvels was the only one of the three to make money from the venture.

Cartuyvels was accused of some unpriestly behavior from time to time which was no impediment to mid-19th century land-dealing.

Others credit him with building a church in St. Marystown, but that seems unlikely. What is more probable is that he was the author or co-author of a deceptive broadside describing Elk County and St. Marys, written to lure Bavarian and Flemish settlers to the little village. He is also known to have made several trips to Europe to recruit colonists.

Of the people who have been associated with St. Marys since 1842, none is more puzzling than **Baron Heinrich von Schroeder**.

Mother Theresa of the Poor School Sisters of Notre Dame and **Bishop Saint John Cardinal Newman** regarded him as an opportunist, charlatan, and con man. Some considered him to have been the colonies most considerable patron.

Von Schroeder was born in Schwerin, Germany in 1805, raised a strict Lutheran and then converted to Catholicism while in Rome, while learning to paint portraits.

Rumor has it, he kidnapped his son after his wife left him and gave the boy to a Danish artist friend to raise. He seems to have then traveled to Munich before drifting into debauchery.

For the remainder of his life, he alternated between licentiousness, and piety.

In August 1845, Benzinger and Eschbach, in need of cash for their land speculation and seeing their kind of guy in the Baron, took him in as a third partner.

It's likely that the Baron never had much money.

Following their alliance, von Schroeder is said to have claimed to be the founder of St. Marys.

A story relates that the Baron invested his fortune in missionary work and died a pauper.

His burial place is obscure.

Some argue that he was buried at St. Vincent Archabbey, while other accounts have him buried in a family vault in the Tyrol.

BAVARIA is a section of Southeast Germany that Tilly and von Pappenheim defended from Protestants during the Thirty Years War. It had been a Duchy, a state, and a Republic. In 1806 Napoleon declared it a kingdom, and his elector, **Maximillia Joseph**, crowned himself king following the example of the Bonaparte. He was succeeded by his son, **King Ludwig I** (Lois Louis), but the Kingdom dissolved after the Bavarian Revolution in 1918 with Ludwig III's exile.

Ludwig's fervent German nationalism brought him into early conflict with his Napoleonic father and the Austrian, Metternich.

His patronage of the arts allowed Munich to serve as the cultural center of Germany. He was also a patron of the Catholic Church, founding the Missionsverein (Louis Mission Society). He was the primary monetary supporter for Saint Marystown in the 1840s.

The Mission Society survived from 1842 to 1921 and provided thousands of dollars to American seminaries, colleges, settlements, and assisted with the labor among native Americans and blacks.

Ludwig and his relation resembled characters from a Strauss or Lehar operetta. "Mad" Ludwig III bankrupted the country building castles and another member of his family who died in a suicide/murder pact with a commoner at Castle Mayerling provided material for a dozen plays and novels.

Ludwig took up with the notorious Irish dancer and actress **Lola Montez** (née Mary Eliza Gilgert).

He appointed her **Gräfin von Landsfeld** (Countess of Landsfeld) and allowed her to assert substantial control over the country.

The King's mistresses were of no concern to Europeans who had grown accustomed to the proclivities of their crowned heads.

At the outset of the Revolutions of 1848 in the German states, she was forced to flee to the United States.

Some argue that the Montez-Ludwig affair to have been Arthur Conan Doyle's inspiration for *A Scandal in Bohemia*, the first Sherlock Holmes story.

In 1844, St. Marystown began to look less like an outpost and more like a village. Father John Neumann visited the colony on several occasions that year.

On one of these visits, the future saint baptized **Xavier Sosenheimer**.

In August 1844, the first marriage in the little settlement was performed.

John Neumann was born in Prachatice, Bohemia (now the Czech Republic) and emigrated to the States in 1836. He was ordained later that year. In 1840 he joined Redemptorists and associated his person with Saint Marystown soon after.

He was of small stature but able and energetic. In 1852, he was named Bishop of Philadelphia, where he constructed many schools.

In 1977 he became the first American to have been canonized (declared a Saint).
In July of 1844, several Redemptorists brothers were sent to the colony. One of their first projects was to dig a canal along Silver Creek to channel water to a sawmill near the Silver-Elk Creeks confluence, an area originally seen as the possible center of St. Marys.

Construction of the Brothers' Sawmill meant that board lumber would be available in the colony.

Meanwhile, back in Baltimore, Mattius Benzinger hired the talented Ignatius Garner as his agent.

A few weeks later, Garner, who was a schoolteacher, musician, linguist, craftsman, and now land agent would marry Julia Weis in Philadelphia.

Within a couple of months, Garner and Father Cartuvals would travel to Bavaria to recruit settlers for Benzinger.

Ignatius Garner's father-in-law, **George Weis**, was another important early St. Marys citizen.

Born in Baden, Germany, he arrived at the colony in 1895 with a large stock of dry goods and set up a shop in the two-story John Walker home. For many years, he would be the principal merchant in St. Marystown and Centreville.

Weis built the 1st stone house in the colony, locating his shop on the 1st floor and a living quarters on the 2nd. The house stands today and is known as the Stackpole-Hall Foundation.

We may assume that it looked much more primitive in 1865 than it does today.

In many ways 1845 was a defining year in the story of St. Marys, for that was when first Catholic Church was built and the first Brewery established.

The two additions to colony provided the Bavarian settlers with two important facets of their culture.

The Church would eventually be a part of a building complex situated in the vicinity of the present-day medical facilities. It would also contain a priest and brother's quarters, barns and sheds, a dwelling for the School Sisters of Notre Dame and a school.

After the Redemptorists and School Sisters left the settlement, the area was then occupied by Benedictines.

Their buildings were crude and resembled other early structures in the colony. The complex would not have been much more than a stone's throw from the Brothers' sawmill and the future Grist Mill which had been situated near the sawmill on the Elk Creek.

An old photo of the compound exists, but the buildings have never been identified. It is not known where the church stood when the photo was taken.

Michael Hans built what would be the first of several small neighborhood breweries. It was located near the Oilwell-Michael streets intersection.

The small creek that supplied the operation with water is still called Brewery Run.

Hans was a town councilman and supervisor. His brewery made him the colonies first manufacturer.

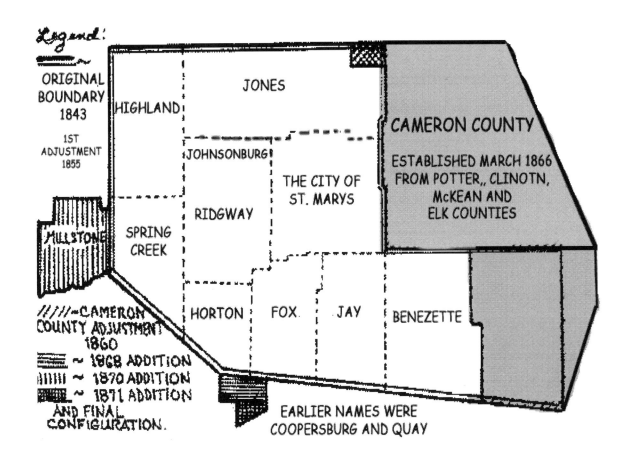

While St. Marystown was experiencing birth pains, Elk County was doing likewise. The county was established four months following the founding of St. Marys from pieces of Jefferson, McKean & Clearfield Counties.

In its present configuration, it's comprised of an area of 814.26 square miles which enclose 10 townships and a city consolidation.

In 1845, Ridgway won the honor of sitting as the County Seat having defeated Wilcox, Brandy Camp, St. Marys and Benezette. Previously, Caledonia was the seat of the first County post office and court proceedings.

101

A map made in 1782, the year the Constitution was ratified, shows the area from Fort Pitt north to Slippery Rock, north to the old state line above Fort Le Boeuf as donation lands.

From Venango west to Towanda, the area encompassing present day Warren, Venanco, Forest, Elk, McKean, Jefferson, Cameron, Potter, Tioga and parts of Bradford, Sullivan and Lycoming counties were all shown as North-Umberland, unknown and rarely visited.

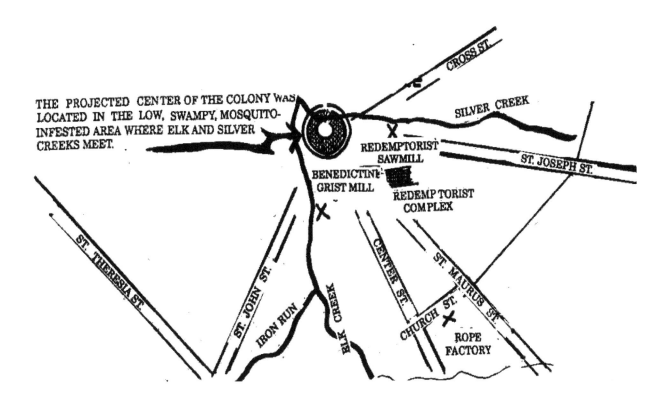

Although Father Alexander had suggested that the settlers locate close one another, they had refused the admonition when Mother Theresa Gerhardinger arrived in St. Marystown in 1845.

At the time, upwards of one hundred families had located to the colony, but there was little evidence of a village.

By 1845, not much of the early Redemptorist Utopian "Wagon Wheel" concept remained.

Census records demonstrate that nearly all the homes to had been situated in the South St. Marys, Center, and Cross Streets areas.

Today, Center, St. Marys, and Maurus streets remain residential areas. The farms which occupied Center and Maurus roads throughout the 1940s are gone, but many of the community's older homes can be found on those streets.
The Cross Street and Ten Cent Run dwellings have vanished without a trace, and the Cross St. Silver Creek bridge utilized by rural delivery men in the 1940s has been

claimed by nature and lost in the undergrowth as is the old lower Cross Street, called the "Pig Farm" road. Up to the mid-50s, it was a popular road for a family stroll.

The mills were the subject of an archeological dig in 1992, a feature of the Sesquicentennial Celebration. One can still walk to the grist mill foundation and view the stones in the Elk Creek riverbed behind what we called the ice cream shop.

In mid-April, Garner and the on and off Redemptorist, Cartuyvels, sailed for Germany to recruit more settlers.

They were then employed as agents of Mattius Benzinger.

For the next six years, along with Garner and Cartuyvals, Jacob Schaut and Baron von Schroeder would travel to Germany to recruit colonists for St. Marystown.

On one of those ventures someone, possibly von Schroder, interested King Ludwig in the struggling colony, and St. Marystown became a beneficiary of the Luis Mission Society.

105

Some 500 Germans are known to have emigrated to the states when Garner and Cartuyvals returned.

Arguably, no more than half of them settled in the St. Marystown colony.

Records have Garner returning on July 15. Others have Father Cartuyvals baptizing Andrew Kaul on July 16, which indicates that perhaps the Redemptorist was not really a member of the first recruiting mission.

Benzinger and Eschbach then took von Schroeder as a partner and signed a land agreement with the Redemptorist order represented by Father Alexander.

JAMES POLK
(1795 - 1849)

The man who followed John Tyler into the American Presidency, **James Polk**, who could not have been more dissimilar. He was reserved, cold, anti-social, stingy, and apparently took no interest in the social problems of the time, some of which included slavery, Know-Nothing bigotry and women's rights. Never-the-less, some historians claim that only George Washington experienced greater political success.

To this day, Polk remains the only Speaker of the House to ever be elected president.

Polk was a believer in and supporter of **MANIFEST DESTINY**.

It was during his single term when the United States accomplished its greatest territorial growth and as covered wagon trains trekked to Oregon, the Mormons founded Utah. With the addition of Texas and Iowa, the American flag would contain thirty stars.

In 1848, with the discovery of gold in California, the West would open, and the population of that Golden state would increase from fifteen thousand to one hundred thousand in just three years.

By the mid-1840s, the anti-Catholic Native American Party, more commonly called the "Know Nothings," were burning Catholic Churches and tar and feathering priests in Boston, New York, Philadelphia, and Baltimore. By 1852, their "American Party" was a significant political force.

Black churches were set aflame throughout the South, and white-robed clansmen burned crosses in the Pennsylvania heartland.

Anti-immigrant legislation was proposed and chants of "America for Americans" persisted.

THE IRISH
POTATO
FAMINE
1845 - 1848

Europe, despite suffering no major wars at the time, was experiencing a series of events which would profoundly affect the German settlement of Saint Marystown in the deep forest of Pennsylvania's Buffalo Swamp.

There was no single cause for The Great Famine during which more than seven-hundred-fifty-thousand Irish would starve to death.

Over-planting, crop disease, absentee landlords, lack of nutritional diversity and political neglect each contributed to the national tragedy.

During this time hundreds of thousands of the Irish fled their island, most of them sailing to the States. This influx of "Papist" Irish, portrayed as only a notch above the Neanderthal, increased "Know Nothing" outrage in the northern coastal cities.

These new immigrants were employed as railroad workers, canal diggers and other menial and laborious occupations.

Following the 1848 Paris Rebellion, many riots and demonstrations took place in Austria and the Germanies, causing the Confederation to disintegrate and motivating a massive German wave of immigration to the United States.

It was on the eve of the Revolution that Karl Marx and Friedrich Engels published the **Manifesto of the Communist Party** with its famous call: "Workers of the world unite. You have nothing to lose but your chains."

Aspects of pioneer life were often described in folk songs, and the immigrant Irish Gandy was no exception.

Our boss's name it was Tom King
He kept a store to rob the men,
A Yankee clerk with ink and pen,
To cheat Pat on the railway

- From **Patrick on the Railroad**

"Drill, Ye Tarriers, Drill" is an American folk song first published in 1888 and attributed to Thomas Casey (words) and later Charles Connolly (music). The song is a work song and makes references to the construction of the American railroads in the mid-19th century.

The boss was a fine man down to the ground.
And he married a lady six-foot round.
She baked good bread and she baked it well,
But she baked that bread just as hard as hell.

So, drill, ye tarriers, drill!
And drill, ye tarriers, drill!
Oh, it's work all day for the sugar in your tay
Down beyond the railway.
So drill, ye tarriers, drill!

Father Czvikovicz was Superior or Vice Urgent, as the head of the Redemptorist order was called in the U.S. This did not stop him from coming to St. Marys and assuming the role of both civic and spiritual leader of a floundering colony.

Between August 1845 and February 1847, when Father Alexander was in St. Marystown, the massive investment jeopardized the future of the Redemptorist order, ultimately causing his recall and replacement as Vice Urgent.

Thereafter, he worked in Louisiana in near exile and did not return to St. Marys for 27 years.

During his Orleans sojourn, Alexander worked with victims of yellow fever and cholera.

In late August 1876, the venerable old Redemptorist returned to St. Mary to visit friends and look over the progress of what was in many ways his town.

While visiting, he offered Sunday mass in a packed "German" church.

Father Alexander Czvikowicz died August 2, 1883, on the Feast of St. Alphonsus, his patron saint and founder of the Redemptorist order.

During Father Alexander's years in the colony, the first school was built near the Redemptorist complex.

It stood in the vicinity of the late Harrison Stackpole's home. There, brother Xavier taught the boys of the colony.

70 years later, the building was used as a sheep cote for the Pilz-Monastery farm.

In 1846 two events took place, which, while neither occurred in St. Marys, must both be listed among the 10 most important happenings in St. Marys history.

That year, the young Father Boniface Wimmer left Munich with 14 laymen and four students for the diocese of Pittsburg where he had been invited to settle.

This man, who would come to be called the "St. Benedict of North America," built a monastery in the states.

From the start, the histories of Saint Vincent Archabbey and St. Marys would be intertwined.

Wimmer was born in hamlet of Thalmassing, Bavaria, and ordained in August 1831.

ARCHABBOT
BONIFACE
WIMMER
O.S.B.
1809 - 1887

In 1847 with his Latrobe Monastery underway, he traveled unaccompanied on horseback through the Buffalo Swamp wilderness to St. Marystown from Indiana, PA.

His journal paints a far from flattering picture of the colony, but he recognized its potential and supplied money, tools, priests, brothers, and influence that brought the Benedictine Sisters to the village.

Wimmer died on Dec. 8, 1887, the anniversary of the founding of St. Marys.

In 1846, the brilliant and energetic Ignatius Garner, land agent for Benzinger and Eschbach in the colony, was sent to Philadelphia as Elk County delegate to meet with officials of the Sunbury and Erie Railroad concerning its completion.

This isn't the place to tell the story of the evolution of the mighty Pennsylvania Railroad, but in 1846 Garner helped set in motion the wheels that were to bring the railroad through St. Marys, contributing to its survival.

With new immigrants and settlers arriving in St. Marystown and the earlier colonists busy building more substantial housing units, clearing land, and establishing farms, it was necessary to provide some temporary housing until more cabins could be built.

What they devised came to be known as the "Holdover House." It was erected circa 1846 and was a three story 30 room log structure situated where the CMF now stands.

It had a common hearth dining area and privy. Water had to be carried from nearby Elk Creek. With 10 to 20 family units being housed, it must have been the scene of continuous argument, noise, and confusion.

In 1846, some colony statistics were assembled. The number of family units was back up to 100 or so with approximately 670 adults and children and approximately one hundred dwellings scattered around. Seventy of these were log cabins. The 1st St. Marys tax assessment was conducted in 1846 by the merchant, George Weis.

115

In 1928, the Elk County Gazette published a list of names purported to be the first settlers. They acknowledged probable discrepancies. Listed are the male members only.

Mathias Wellendorf	Francis Cordes	Wm. Borgman
Adolph Stockman	Charles Schreiber	Michael Derleth
John Walker	Valentine Hesperline	Michael Steigerwald
Lorenz Stockman	Louis Vollmer	Martin Herbstritt
Herman Koch	Jacob Schaut	Frederick Spohener
Joseph Stockman	Adam Vollmer	Bartol Geier
Julius Vornbaum	Xaverius Biberger	Anton Koch
John Stockman	Francis Tegler	John Sosenheimmer
Anton Fochtman	Bonifatus Schmand	George Hasselman
Joseph Diehl	Clemenz Osterman	John Haas
Anton Ewes	John Albert	John B. Hast
Michael Diehl	F.X. Mueller	F. Haas
Francis Kallar	Nicholas Reimel	Jacob Didlot
Nicholas Hill and father	Francis Renner	J.H. Weichman
Adam Kinges		

Many of these names had left the colony by the time the first census was taken.

People often ask, "Were there any Indians here?"

Well, there weren't many, at least not in the last three centuries, but some of the old residents of Benzinger recalled occasional groups passing the settlement outskirts.

"The Maid of Blue Rock" and Jim Jacobs are Elk County's two best known Native Americans, but little is known about either on

117

Jacobs was a half-breed hunter who may have been descended from Red Jacket, Corn Planter or both.

Tradition has it that he killed the last native elk along the banks of the Clarion at a date that ranges from as early as 1843 to 1867.

Rumors of the wood bison clearing large tracts in Pennsylvania (Clearfield) are probably not true because no skeletal remains were ever found. However severe winters did occasionally drive moose, lynx, and wolverines into unsettled, colonial Pennsylvania.

Black bears and cougars are two large north American mammals known to have been native to all the lower 48 states. Cougars have been gone since the 1890s, but people still claim sightings; however, such is hard to believe as no tracks or carcasses have been recorded in the last century.

Wolves and bobcats were not uncommon in the early years of the colony, and the big weasels (fishers, otters, martins) still haunted the Elk County deep woods and riverbanks.

In 1847 a census was taken in the colony, and interesting things can be learned from it.

There were 186 scattered dwellings with 223 family units, which probably means that the "Holdover House" was in use.

The census shows two stone houses, both on St. Marys Rd. They would have been the Weis (Meisel) home/store, and the Bartolt Geyer farmhouse, known to have been the first stone house built on the Settler's Trail to Marienstadt from Centreville.

Five years after the colony was established, there were still 27 log dwellings on Michael St., 21 on Center, 21 in the Cross St- Joseph St. area, and 17 on St. Marys St.

These were likely intended as temporary shelters when built and would make most of today's hunting camps seem modern.

119

The total number of recorded souls in the colony in 1847 was 964.

Of these, 510 were children, and an unknown number were elderly.

It would be several decades before the colony would create a rest home and housing for the less fortunate.

The census also identified most of the male colonists as farmers, shop keepers, wood workers and craftsmen, among whom several were cordwainers, as shoemakers were then called.

One of these was one sabot (wooden shoe) maker.

1847 marked the arrival of five members of the Order of Poor School Sisters of Notre Dame.

It is one of the most interesting but least studied events in early St. Marys History.

The sisters discovered they would have to wear secular attire while traveling in the young nation.

One nun, Sister Emmanuel, rarely healthy, likely died from dysentery and was buried in a country cemetery along the long, lonely forest trail from Harrisburg to St. Marystown.

The

Redemptorist fathers in Baltimore had advised the sisters not to travel to St. Marys but to return to Germany. The men who had asked them to come, Schroeder or Cartuyvels, had neither requested nor had received permission for the School Sisters to establish themselves in the Pittsburgh Diocese.

St. Mary's men celebrated the arrival of the school sisters on August 15, 1847.

The Sisters discovered to their dismay that the Redemptorist rule prevented the priests and brothers from much association with the nun orders.

Their living quarters were also found to be a disaster.

Mother Theresa Gerhardinger was 60 years old
when she arrived in America with five young
novitiates. She helped to revive the order 14 years
before but had no authority approved by Rome or
her superiors in Germany.

Her letters, especially to Father Siegert, the
spiritual advisor in Bavaria, gave one of the best
eye-witness accounts of early Saint Marys yet to be
discovered.

Mother Gerhardinger's letters
abound with descriptions of
poverty, hunger, remoteness,
poor soil, and bad weather.

To her, it seemed apparent that success for the colony was unlikely.

In July of 1848, Mother Theresa retuned to Munich to complete work on her order's Holy Rule.

She left behind four sisters to teach the young St. Marys girls. Her letters provide a vivid, personal portrait of King Ludwig, Father John Neumann, and the peculiar Baron von Schroeder.

Mother of the American Order of School Sisters of Notre Dame, Mary Caroline Friess (1824-1892), was just 23 when she accompanied Mother Theresa Gerhardinger to America after Theresa was appointed superior general of her Orders for life.

Gerhardinger appointed Sister M. Caroline Vicar General in America.

Mother Coroline founded a Milwaukee Mother House in 1850 and by 1942, the order would have established close to 500 schools in North and Central America.

Since we began the telling of the St. Marystown Saga, the colony had thus transformed from an idea into a reality and was about to celebrate its fifth birthday.

There were nearly 1000 souls living in the colony, and they had erected a sawmill, church, brewery, general store, and Post Office.

Although it resembled a frontier crossroad, civilization was moving into St. Marystown. The first piano and sewing machine (invented in 1842) were laboriously hauled into the colony by way of the Milesburg Turnpike in 1847.

Nuns taught the girls, and brothers taught the boys. Father Alexander had resurveyed the colony and convinced Benzinger and Eschbach to assume the debt. Meanwhile, Ignatius Garner promoted St. Marys like no one else had before or since.

It was beginning to look like the colony might make it. It is in the folk songs of America that we get some of our most vivid pictures of the period.

When I got there, the hills were steep.
It would make any tender-hearted person weep
To hear me cuss and pop my whip
And watch leaders pull and slip.

-The Ox-Driver's Lament

We all know who the Forty-Niners were, but we don't often hear of the politically incorrect Forty-Eighters.

Following the German Revolution of 1848, many German-American intellectuals began calling themselves **FORTY-EIGHTERS.** They adopted the the slogan, "Freiheit ist meine!" and joined the Know-Nothings in burning churches, tarring and feathering priests, stoning nuns, and desecrating religious objects.

The working-class German laborers and farmers were rarely a part of these activities and often the victims.

A young Springfield, Illionois lawyer, Abraham Lincoln, would remark at the time:

"Although we had declared all men to be created equal, we meant all but negroes.

When the Know-Nothings get control, it will read "all men are created equal, except negroes, and foreigners, and catholics."

In February 1848, the treaty of Guadalupe Hildago was signed with Mexico after an on and off again series of military engagements over thirty years.

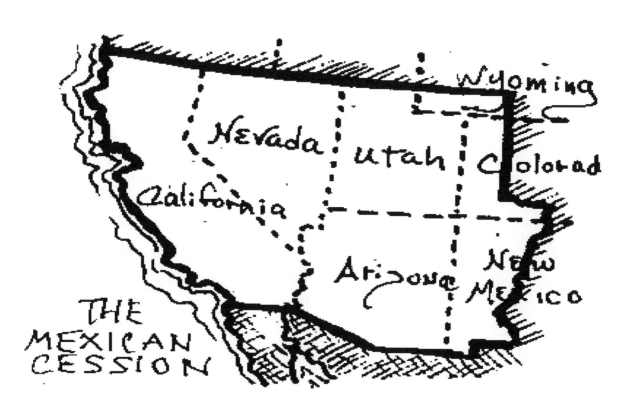

In 1848 Benzinger and Eschbach acquired another partner in the person of William A. Stokes, a prominent lawyer from Philadelphia.

Stokes moved his family to St. Marystown that year into a section to be called Roselay Rd. after his wife.

He then began to build a large home in the Roselay section, but his beloved but physically weak wife died less than a year after, and the uncompleted house was abandoned.

The broken-hearted barrister sold his interests in the colony and returned to Philadelphia.   It was then that the Belgian Redemptorist Father Cartuvels became a full partner.

129

After lawyer Stokes left Saint Marystown, others arrived almost daily. Many names still prominent can still be found in the colony: Kaul-Pistner-Goetz-Brunner-Lion-Ritter-Kraus-Loeffler-Forester-Schlimm-Volk-Geitner-Decker-Wegemer-Krellner-Luhr-Regard-Schad-Keller-Schaeffer-Butsch-Eckl.

BERNARD WEIDENBOERNER, a cobbler, had arrived in 1845. He and his wife raised twelve children, which blossomed to sixty second-generation descendants. He exchanged his shoe-maker shop with the Church Committee in 1848 for land on the other side of the road.

Saint Mary's Church was built on his property.

The young multi-lingual teacher, Ignatius Garner, who returned to St. Marys in 1845 as land agent for the Benzinger-Eschbach venture, was appointed first postmaster for Benzinger that same year.

In 1846 he became the colony's first Justice of the Peace.

In 1848 St. Marystown held its first popular election.

The indefatigable Ignatius Garner was elected first Burgess of the little village on April 29. The St. Marys Ballot Box, dating from that election, can be seen at the St. Marys Historical Society.

It was also in 1848 that the village of St. Marystown was incorporated into Borough.

131

Of interest is that although the colony was then officially a borough, the Benzinger Twp. School District would remain the only St. Marys school system for many years.

The Post Office designation, Benzinger, would
Last for nearly thiry yearss.

In April of 1849, Congress gave civilians the right to organize local militia units. By May 20th, German settlers in St. Marys had dragged out their muskets and formed the Elk County Rifle Company.

This organization would reorganize as the Elk Artillery No.1 roughly ten years later.

The early militia would eventually become Company H., 16th Regiment, PA National Guard.

Every officer in the unit in 1849 had a family name that was still familiar locally a hundred years later, e.g., Schoening, Schaut, Bucheit, Rettger, Schaeffer, Weis, Eckl, Dill, and Jesberger.

Gerhart Schoening was a merchant and builder who came to St. Marys during the first years. He was the first captain of the Elk Rifles.

His son, **Frederick,** reorganized the unit as the Ridgway Rifles in 1874 and was Captain in Command when they assisted putting down the Pittsburg riots of 1877.

Governor Pattison granted him the title of colonel when he served as the Governor's aide. When age forced his retirement, his son **Leo** took command of the "Rifles."

Sometime in 1849, the colony's first newspaper was published.

No copy of **The Elk County Republican** is known to have survived. It is doubtful that it ever printed a second edition.

In late November of 1849, following the unfortunate exile of the energetic visionary, Father Alexander, the Redemptorists abandoned their efforts in Saint Marystown to stabilize their diminishing resources.

The School Sisters, never very secure or comfortable in their Saint Marystown mission, also left for greener pastures in the rapidly developing Midwest.

700 acres of Redemptorist holdings, which had been granted to the order to build church and school, would be built reverted back to Benzinger and Eschbach.

They quickly turned the land over to Michael O'Connor, Bishop of Pittsburg, in the hope that he would send priests to the colony. Most of the settlers had been lured to St. Marys with the promise of priests, churches, and schools.

Their spiritual needs were real.

Within days after the withdrawal of the Redemptorists, a group of settlers drew up a resolution which accused the order of being more interested in making money than in religious service.

135

When visiting priests from Pittsburgh or St. Vincent visited the colony, they were sometimes held hostage.

It was not uncommon for priests who passed through Catholic quarters and settlements without resident clergy to be kidnapped until they said mass, performed marriages, and baptized children.

In a letter from Mother M. Theresa Gerhardinger, written to a German Bishop in 1850, Theresa expressed her disapproval of the sisters leaving in her absence despite the poor living and teaching conditions and the fact that no American Bishop had accepted them.

She wrote that St. Marys had been very dear to her, and she would never forget it.

After the departure of the Redemptorists, the settlers contacted Father Boniface and requested that he send priests to serve St. Marys.

Wimmer, who had expressed interest in the colony, dispatched Father Benedict Heindl and Father Andrew Zugriegel to Saint Marystown.

Father Alexander's hasty departure in late 1849 not only deprived the settlement of spiritual leadership, the Redemptorist visionary had also provided Saint Marystown with stable civic leadership.

There was much worry and concern in the snowbound cabins during the winter of 1849.

During the same winter, what was likely the settlement's first fire occurred when the Holdover House burned to the ground.

In 1849, the major event in the settlement was the departure of the Redemptorists and school sisters.

In the rest of America, there was a great rush of fortune seekers and adventurers to the California territory.

On January 24th, 1848, Scotch carpenter **James W. Marshall** discovered what looked like quality gold while cleaning out his mill race for his employer. Johan Augustus one of the most interesting but little-known personages in pioneer America.

Sutter was a soldier of fortune of Swiss parentage who set himself up as a self-appointed emperor of the "New Helvetia" in the American occupied Mexican territory. After Sutter and Marshall proved what they found was gold with an encyclopedia and a druggist scale, he requested title to the land. It was still Mexican territory so the title it wasn't granted.

Eleven days later, California became an American territory.

Although the rumor of gold traveled eastward slowly and was not taken very seriously everywhere, occurrences like an entire garrison at Monterey deserting the ranks to look for gold is a fact of history.

The Gold Rush had begun, and tens of thousands of forty-niners rushed overland by wagon train.

Sutter's land was soon overrun by fortune hunters and died nearly broke. Tens of thousands of 49ers rushed overland by wagon train or around Cape Horn.

We don't know how many, if any, young men from Saint Marystown succumbed to the "Gold Fever" epidemic that swept the nation.

Polk was the first American President not to seek re-election. He was succeeded by the Whig hero of the Mexican War,

General Zachary Taylor (1774-1850). Taylor died mid-term, serving just sixteen months.

During his brief presidency, he displayed wisdom, courage, and leadership. Despite being a southern slave owner, he made it known that he'd direct the Army to prevent any southern states from seceding.

The slavery issue was heating up in the states, and the great compromise of 1850 resulted from a series of debates between the greatest men in American history not to become president: Calhoun, Clay, Seward, Douglass, and Webster.

On another burner, the issue of women's rights was boiling with the appearance of the periodical, Lilly, published by the temperance and female and rights advocate Ms.Amelia Jenks Bloomer (1818-1894).

141

A sudden death during the fierce slavery debate raises the question as to whether Taylor was poisoned by his political enemies. In 1991, his remains were exhumed and examined by forensic experts. They found no trace of poison.

At mid-century, the United State was seventy-four years old and was beginning to be taken seriously by other nations. Poe and Hawthorne had status in the international literary community, and England and the U.S.A. had signed a treaty guaranteeing the neutrality of a Central American canal joining the oceans.

Continued civil unrest in Europe contributed to larger numbers of immigrants to coming to America.

Saint Marystown at midcentury was in one of its darkest periods. Father Alexander Czvikovicz, the great patron and inspiration of the colony, had been sent packing to Louisiana, and the Redemptorist order and the School Sisters had abandoned the colony, leaving it without religious services and teachers.

Rumors of the impending division of the vast Pittsburgh Diocese with a new Bishopric in Erie were more constant. No one in the colony had any idea how this how this might affect the questionable state-of-affairs regarding Diocesan status.

As Ignatius Garner's commitment to St. Marys and its citizenry grew, so did an estrangement between him and his employers, John Eschbach and Mathias Benzinger.

Letters from Eschbach and Benzinger suggest their agent was being far too lenient with the settlers and neglected the collection of outstanding debts.

With the Redemptorist' departure, the sawmill was idled. However, by 1850, several others would be active.

There were, however, still a few neighborhood breweries operating.
Although a census had been taken, taxes levied, and an election held, many new settlers and visitors still

marveled at the primitive conditions in St. Marystown and allotted little hope for the long-term survival of the community.

Other than the makeshift church, the religious complex sat empty and deserted, a victim of time and vandalism.

FIRE !!

was the great enemy of pioneer America. Examinations of early village and town records indicate that were often subject to destructive conflagrations.

Court houses, town halls, barns, churches, livery stables, mills, and often entire city blocks frequently were subject to devastating fires.

Open hearths, candles, oil lamps, over-heated wood stoves, uncured hay, and steam locomotives were likely the cause of massive blazes.

The fire companies were usually only bucket brigades that at best possessed a hose reel and hand pump.

On May 10th, 1851, the makeshift wooden church burned to the ground.

The fire was likely started by an untended candle.

When the wooden framed church burned, the colony's only place of worship went up in smoke.

145

Following so closely after the departure of the School Sisters and Redemptorists, the settler's morale sank to an all-time low.

No priests were in residence when the church burned, but the place had also served as their living quarters.

The colony's first organ which had been designed and built by Ignatius Garner was also lost in the fire.

Boniface Wimmer arrived in America, planning to train priests. His idea met ridicule.

Bishop O'Connor of the Pittsburgh Diocese would eventually offer Wimmer and his followers the Sportsman's Hall in Latrobe, a primitive log structure where a parish had been established in 1790.

Later, the sounds of monks reciting the Divine Office would be heard in the old log cabin (St. Vincent Parish).

The Young Benedictines nearly starved and froze during the first winter, and the situation looked worse in 1847 when Father Peter Lechner arrived from Bavaria with a bit of money and 20 young immigrants seeking Holy Orders.

147

By early 1848, the monks sawed their own lumber, ground grain, fabricated bricks and baked their bread.

On October 29, they would lay the cornerstone for the complex that would become the motherhouse of Western Monasticism in the young nation.

In August 1851, Father Wimmer, who had been interested in the Saint Marystown experiment since arriving in Western Pennsylvania, sent Fathers Benedict and Maurus to take up residence in the colony.

From that day on, Saint Marys would be a Benedictine community.

148

The arrival of the Benedictines greatly improved the attitude in the community.

Here was an order committed to the colony which would bring priests, teachers, craftsmen, and artisans to Saint Marystown. The priests and brothers attended to the holdings formerly held by the Redemptorists and became permanent residents in St. Marys.

In the winter of 1851, plans were underway to begin the construction of a church.

Some researchers believe that the plans for the Saint Marys Church may have originated in Garner's native Alsace Lorraine.

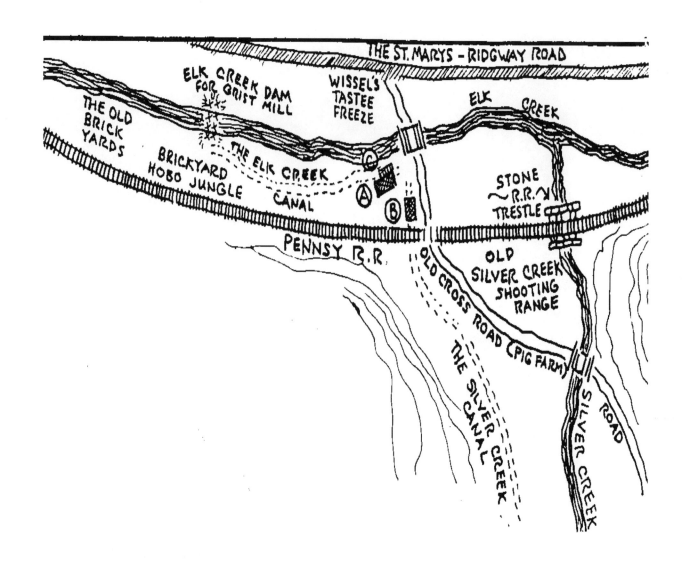

We don't know that the Redemptorists erected both a sawmill and a gristmill, but evidence suggests the Benedictines operated at least one mill of each kind in Silver Creek Valley in the 1850s.

A. Approximate site of grist mill
B. Approximate site of sawmill
C. Cut foundation stones can be seen in the creek bed

1851 was the 9th year that the Saint Marys residents would celebrate Christmas since forming the colony. To their dismay, the church had burned, and their dwellings were still substandard.

However, there were a few baking and cooking facilities where delicious German holiday food could be prepared. Some of the settlers had used valuable space in their luggage areas to transport creche figurines from Europe to the colony.

151

Many Bavarian colonists were skilled craftsmen and woodworkers who maintained a tradition of homemade villages and hand-carved figures being placed beneath the beloved "Tannenbaum."

On the 51st day after Easter in 1852, following the celebration of mass, the population of Saint Marystown gathered to start clearing land halfway between Saint Benedict and Saint Maurus Streets on the former Weidenboerner property.

The villagers cleared the land and dug the foundation.

Different sections of the village were assigned certain days to work.

153

Nine 62 feet long beams cut for the ceiling joists were felled in winter weather to reduce dry rot. They were broad axed to the length to 12 x 12. These continue to support the structure to this day.

The sandstone outside walls were cut at a quarry on a hill just north of the building site. The lime derived from strata discovered on the same hillside.

Men walked or rode in oxen-pulled wagons to the church site on their designated day.

The "heavenly house father" remunerated their efforts.

The church work was both difficult and dangerous, as they used no motorized equipment, and block & tackle was in short supply.

Ignatius Garner and Father Benedict Heindl supervised the job, but they too donned boots and overalls and joined in the labors.

The marks of broadaxes and adzes are clearly visible wherever the original wood is to be seen in the Saint Marystown Church.

Among the carpenter-craftsmen were lay brothers sent from Saint Vincent to assist with the construction of the house of worship.

The axes, adzes, chisels, picks, etc. used in the construction were brought to George Weigel for sharpening and repair.

He was the only blacksmith in the colony and was also paid in heavenly credits.

Early maps of Saint Marystown depict the area to the southwest, called New Munster. To the east a section had been named New Brabant.

The most curious section was labeled New Flanders, an idea of Father Alexander Czvikovicz to locate a settlement of Belgian glass blowers near the Jones Township line where Crooked Creek crosses the highway.

The colony never took off, but a few Flemish glass blowers and other Belgians did settle in the colony. Heary is said to be one of the names still prominent from this episode of the community's past.

Many local glass blowers who worked in Dr. Pierce's Fourth Street bottle plant and the early glass novelty would gain employment in what was Sylvania, an incandescent lightbulb factory.

Many Belgian immigrants did settle in the Rosely Rd/Eschbach Rd area, and Brusselles Street was likely named after Belgium's national capital.

When Father Boniface Wimmer made his first trip to St. Marystown in 1847, despite the area having been that of mud and brush, he compared it to Munich. And felt that the colony was laid out on a grand a scale but would never achieve much growth without a navigable river or canal. He did express optimism with the Philadelphia and Erie Railroad's tracks through the Saint Marystown area.

Although Wimmer had misgivings about the Marienstadt location, he wrote that he would recommend German immigrants of modest means to settle there. He let it be known that he intended to build a Benedictine Monastery nine miles from the settlement.

This land was sixteen miles in the Williamsville area on the Milesburg/Smethport turnpike, one half mile into McKean County.

Father Wimmer's grand monastery plan for this section never was realized.

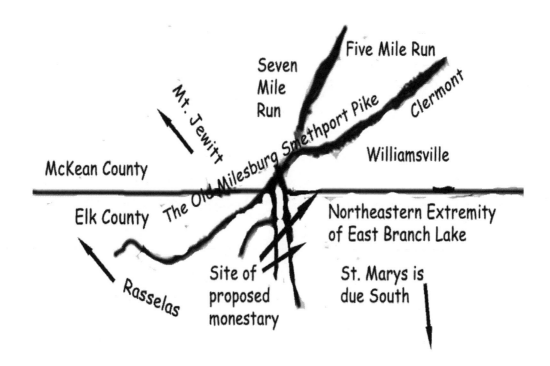

On June 8, 1952, work on the new church had progressed enough for the cornerstone to be laid with appropriate ceremony. Father Boniface Wimmer traveled from Saint Vincent to be celebrant.

Although no one realized it, an event of far greater community significance than the cornerstone laying took place a month later. On July 22nd, 1852, three Benedictine nuns from the Saint Walburga convent in Eichstadt, Germany, arrived to take up residence in Sancta Marienstadt.

The nuns made a six-day journey north from Saint Vincent by farm wagon and shank's mare. They were the first of their order to come to America.   Some believe that that they came at the invitation of Father **Albert Wimmer**

According to traditional lore, the first monk to see them ran to the rest of the community crying to his brother monks that "A wagonload of trouble has arrived."

When the school sisters arrived in 1847, they found their quarters to be nearly in ruins.

In 1852, the three Benedictine Sisters found those same quarters to be even more decrepit.

The Benedictine nuns had been promised much by Father Wimmer, who lured them to the community. The same had been done to the school sisters by Baron von Schroeder. The sisters would soon learn that the quarters were just one of their troubles.

Living conditions were unendurable by today's standards. The quarters were cold, and the nuns subsisted on hard bread with spreads of any kind. Black coffee was breakfast, while broth and potatoes served as their main meals. Blackberries were the only fruit.

Tiny pieces of meat were a rare treat and not served more than twice a week. Holidays were celebrated with mush, lacking both milk and sugar.

In short order, the three sisters from the cloistered convent in Bavaria became involved in the daily life of Sancta Marienstadt.

Their early efforts with the young girls of the settlement were the start of the much-honored St. Benedict's academy.

Soon, they would be teaching young boys and so began a long tenure of sister educators.

Mother Benedicta (Sybilla) Riepp   6/20/1825 - 3/15/1862

Founder of the American branch of the Benedictine Sisterhood, she was appointed superior of the American Mission at 27 years of age.

During the next decade, she would endure much hardship and controversy and found 7 convents before dying of tuberculosis at 36.

The history of the great stand-off between Wimmer and Sister Benedicta is one of the least-known stories of our past as well as one that the Great Abbot's advocates wish would be forgotten.

The Abbot was not above diverting monies sent to the sisters by the Louis Mission Society to his own ends.

He demanded jurisdiction over the sister's money, admissions, elections, discipline, and monastic directives.

The monk Abbot met an anomaly in Sr. Benedicta because male dominance in all church matters had been accepted for centuries – but, the young sister superior would not have it. She pleaded her case back at St. Walburgas in Bavaria where she was treated as a pariah.

Eventually, several American and European Bishops and at least one Curia member would take up her cause.

In 1859, a ruling was made denying Wimmer every point of contention and placing the future of the American sisterhoods in the jurisdiction of the respective dioceses.

Father Boniface directed the convents not to welcome Sister Benedicta back when she returned to the states, but welcome her they did.

Mother Evangelista of the recently established convent in St. Cloud, MN, took her in, and she spent her final years in the convent.

Mother Benedicta Riepp is unknown to many, but she was one of the great unsung heroines of the conflict that womanhood has waged in its effort to achieve greater equality in the world.

 Despite adversity, the two teaching orders of Catholic nuns trace their American origin to the early days of the backwoods settlement of Sancta Marienstadt.

Although the School Sisters moved on after two years, they served as the community's first teachers, and Saint Marystown was their initial stop.

The Benedictine nuns, who arrived three years later, remained to establish a Motherhouse which would germinate into dozens of convents, monasteries & schools in the Western Hemisphere.

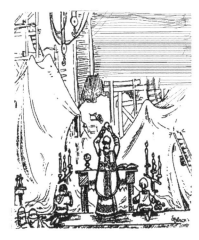 On Dec. 8th, 1853, the 11th Anniversary of the founding of Saint Marystown, the first mass was said in the unfinished church. In 1853, The National Catholic Council, located in Baltimore, MD, broke up the Pittsburgh Diocese.

The settler's fears for the colony's religious future were finally put to rest when the newly elevated Bishop, **Joshua M. Young**, visited Saint Marystown in July.

He blessed the new church and praised the achievements of the settlers.

165

The bishop of the new Diocese, who was himself a convert to the Catholic faith, celebrated the colony's first pontifical High Mass, preaching in German and English before touring the young colony on horseback.

AT ONE TIME THE FARMERS PARKED THEIR TEAMS AND BUGGIES IN SHELTERS BEHIND THE BREWERY WHEN THEY CAME INTO MASS ON SUNDAY MORNINGS.

THE WINDFELDER BREWERY
CENTER ST. ABOUT 1850.

During the early years of the colony, Saint Marystown men worked as woodsmen in nearby communities as coal, clay, and wood products were yet to be exploited.

There was a time when farmers parked their teams and buggies in the shelters behind the brewery when they came to mass on Sunday mornings.

Sometime around 1850, **Joseph Windfelder** opened a second brewery on Beer Creek (Brewery Run). It stood on the site of the present-day Legion where a nearby alley connected Center and Maurus streets.

The Center Street enterprise would be owned by the Luhrs.

There were few common commodities any more valuable than rope in the mid-1800s. Spikes and nails were also expensive, hard to find, and usually handmade.

Wire was even rarer, and a vast amount of rope was in demand for construction, farming, and the sailing trade, especially on the frontiers.

Rope walks were long, strong, and stretched out on spinning wheels.

167

Little is known of this early local enterprise. Benedictine letters and the Wimmer diaries indicate that Ignatius Garner influenced a Mr. Bechtel to start such an operation. It was located on lower Church Street, and the sisal or hemp was grown between Mill and Center Streets.

Father Ruppert Seidenbusch was another famous churchman living in the early Saint Marystown.

In 1853, he organized the colony's first fraternal society **Sanct Johannes Verin**, (The St. John Society). It was essentially a mutual benevolent insurance society that paid sick or injured members a small weekly stipend.

The first meeting was held in the log home of Michael "Bierhans" Hans on North Saint Michael Street. Hans was the town's first brewer and a pillar of the church and community.

The first society president was **Edward Babel**, who would serve as Burgess in 1855 and give his name to Babylon, and amusement park and brewery above Silver Creek

169

Konle Michael,
Haberbosch Xaver,
Breindel John,
Koller Xaver,
Ables John B.,
Brunner Michael,
Gerg Anton,
Stephan Henry.
Heindel John,
Selle George,
Heumenböl Joseph,
Schwarzfischer John,
Schauer Joseph,
Wacker John,
Wesniger Lorenz,
Dippold Andreas,
Auman Anton,
Schmidt George,
Fuchs Wolfgang,
Cerbs Christian,
Jesberger Adam,

Dietl Christoph,
Elmbeck Ludwig,
Schirser Philipp,
Ehrig Xaver,
Malison Jacob,
Beimel George,
Beimel John,
Märtz George,
Hammer George,
Haberberger Clemen
Emet F. X.,
Plßner Adam,
Nicholaus Martin,
Essig Frank,
Schreiter John,
Werner Joseph,
Bauer Anton,
Glaß Andreas,
Geitner John,
Krigel John,
Bauer George,

Hauber Sebastian
Bauer Louis C.,
Werneth August,
Decker George,
Löffler Aloysius,
Schmitt Joseph,
Fello Martin,
Weigel George,
Konle Jacob,
Dieß Joseph,
Vollmer John,
Breindel Simon,
Schuller Joseph,
Gerer Adam,
Kraus Jacob,
Weisenhof John,
Dewald Nikolas,
Luhr Franz,
Krellener George,
Ehrig Frank,
Kraus John,

The early membership lists of St. John's Society are a valuable historical resource, for nearly every adult male in the settlement appears on them

Later in 1855, the energetic **Father Rupert** organized the Saint Joseph Society to provide financial and physical support to the new church. At the time of this writing, it still exists and is the community's longest lived-layman's organization.

Fr. Rupert Seidenbusch went on to become another star on the Saint Vincent crown.

He became the first Abbot of the Saint John Benedictine Abbey in Minnesota, the Vicar Apostolic of that state, and the first Bishop of the Diocese of Saint Cloud Minnesota.

Many of the surnames of the first settlers are still with us. Some have already been listed.
Many more will be.

Louis Vollmer was born in Kandl, Bavaria in 1818 and was elected to the position of Assessor in 1846.

He served as School Director, Justice of the Peace, County Commissioner, and Lime Kiln & Brickyard owner. In 1867 he became one of the organizers and partners of the Saint Marys Bank.

He was also the first elected official in St. Marystown.

Wendel Lion (10/29/1822 – 2/2/1878) was "The First Lawman," a shoemaker by trade, and the village's first constable.

He served with the 172nd Pennsylvania Volunteers during the War between the States and is buried in the Saint Marys Cemetery.

Anton Hanhauser arrived at the colony in 1850 and lived in St. Marys until his death 17 years later.

He built and operated the Philadelphia House which later became The Franklin Hotel.

Bernard Weidenboerner was another shoemaker who was born in Germany. He came to St. Marys in 1845 and lived here until his death in 1886.

He left 12 children and 42 grandchildren.

Notwithstanding construction records from the Church, tax papers, a census, and some baptismal records, little documentation referencing the mid-1850s exists.

Philip Stephann is said to have operated a distillery in Saint Marystown during those years.

The first of several fires occurred at the Benedictine Grist Mill circa 1852.

Near the same time, three houses burned on South Saint Marys Street. These disasters devastated the hard-pressed colony.

 A stagecoach line operating between Clearfield and Olean travelled through Saint Marys in the 1850s by way of the Milesburg Turnpike and made a daily stage stop at an inn located in the Pumpkin Hill vicinity, near the entrance to the East Branch Dam.

There were several hotels operating in Saint Marystown in the 1850s.

What was most likely the town's first coal mine is believed to have been opened by "One-Eyed" Miller.

The mine's opening was on "Priest's Land," likely situated on the Fritz residence on the Johnsonburg Road.

Throughout the next decade, more mines would go into operation.

In 1846, **Michael Decker's** family left Germany and landed in the port city of Baltimore. There, he became involved with the German Catholic Brotherhood. Shortly afterwards, the family made the trek to Saint Marystown. Although they had six children, just two boys survived infancy.

George would later marry **Katherine Weigel** and raise a large family. Many of his descendants still reside in St. Marys.

The other son was named, Michael, after his father. This boy received a calling to the priesthood when he was young. By 1850, at the age of 11, he and two **Pilz** brothers (distant relatives of this writer and the first of many Benedictine priests) walked 125 miles from Saint Marystown to Saint Vincent, carrying bread, and clothes for the semester. The future Father Decker walked back and forth for eight years.

Michael Decker Sr. was a hard-working farmer whose wife of ten years worked with him in the fields. Around 1856 he built a small, crude chapel on his land. after promising to construct the chapel were he to recover from a back injury stemming falling from a tree. Through the years, the chapel would be the scene of frequent processions and devotions as the community gathered to pray for rain or their sons away at war. In 1984, a direct descendent of Michael Decker was married there.

To this day, Decker's Chapel remains open to visitors 365 days a year.

The young Michael Decker completed his studies for the priesthood in Brooklyn. He was an eloquent speaker in both English and German, composed church music, and played many instruments. A competent horseman, he made regular visits to Pithole, a rough town in Pennsylvania. He constructed several churches in the Erie Diocese and was vested a Monsignor in 1904.

His funeral in 1913 was the largest ever held in St. Marys although he never served in the town.

**Monsignor
Michael Decker
(1839-1913)**

Along with Michael Decker, the **Pilz** boys made the trek to Latrobe several times.

The two Pilz boys were a bit older than Mike Decker and would become the colony's first Benedictine priest-monks, establishing a local tradition that would entail one young Saint Marystown man having been ordained every two years. On a per capita basis, this likely makes Saint Marystown the most fruitful Benedictine community in North America.

Father Gerad and **Placidus** (Peter and John Pilz) said their first masses in the new Saint Marystown Church in May 1859. Gerard became a noted scholar and translator, and Placidus was pastor of the St. Marys Church (1885-1888). Their boyhood pal, Mike Decker, read his first mass here in Saint Marystown 1862.

Andrew Hintenach O.S.B, who was not a child of the colony, read his first mass in the Saint Marys Church. He would eventually be elevated to Archabbot.

A few were also ordained as Seculars, Jesuits, Franciscans, etc.
Here are some of the best known:

R.T. Reverend **Anthony Schulers** born on Mill Street in 1848
became the first Bishop of El Paso, Texas, in 1914.

Commander Charles Hacherl was USN, Chaplain of All Naval
and Marine flying units in the South Pacific. He was also a
WWII official observer on the USS Missouri during the
Japanese Surrender, and the National Chaplain of the U.S.
Catholic War Vets. Born on South Saint Marys Road, he was
one of 14 children.

Dr. Gerald Campbell, a distinguished historian, was
named President of Georgetown, University in 1960.
He was born on Neubert Street.

THE ST. MARYSTOWN SAGA ---

As the north central Pennsylvania colony was experiencing growing pains in the 1850s, the young nation was doing likewise.

Millard Fillmore (1850-1853) became the 13th president following the untimely death of Zachary Taylor.

He was a strong supporter of the compromise on slavery and replaced Taylor's cabinet with men who supported it. Today, many historians list him as one of our least competent presidents.

Fillmore was succeeded by the handsome compromise candidate, **Franklin Pierce** (1853-1857) who, like Fillmore, was unable to stabilize the rapidly expanding nation.

His term was marked by domestic tragedy. His wavering on slavery infuriated both the North and the South. His support of immigrants stimulated the formation of the "Know Nothing" party.

American was indeed entering dangerous waters.

During Fillmore's term in 1851-52-53, one the books that changed the world was released.

It was entitled Uncle Tom's Cabin and written by Harriet Beecher Stowe (1811-1896).

In 1855, during the Pierce Presidency, Frederick Douglass (1818? – 1895) published "My Bondage and My Freedom."

Douglass was a former slave and spokesman for American blacks.

The fugitive slave act and the Supreme Court's Dred Scott decision, arguably one the Court's most notorious acts, increased hostility between the North and the South.

In Kansas violence erupted between pro and anti-slavery groups.

The drumbeat of war grew nearer.

The Aristocracy and Saint Marystown:

At the end of the American Revolution, the victors took a fervent stand against the retention of royal titles or any form of aristocracy. In most of Europe, a general sordidness clouded many of the old royal houses, and in France a few decades earlier, the numbers of First and Second Estate members had decreased via dates with madame Guillotine. Saint Marystown was, however, assisted by a small-time king and had close ties with three barons, the lowest order of the Knighted class.

The barons, a German, and two Belgians involved themselves with the early colony. The shadowy von Schroeder, sidekick of Eschbach and Benzinger, visited often but never took up residence. It is said that he often told Europeans that he owned Saint Marystown.

Baron Cartuvals was a brother of the Redemptorist, Father Louie. Little is known about him, but he did reside in St Marystown for a time. Baron von Ersel is the only one of "blue bloods" to be buried in the St. Marystown Cemetery.

Chevalier Charles von Ersel, a Belgian, arrived in Saint Marystown in 1849 searching for better health. The land he bought from Benzinger Road came to be known as White Barn when the Nobleman put up a large white barn on the property.

Township School Number 5, located in the area, became known as Whitebarn School, and was later moved to the Bucktail Trail. At the time of this writing the barn is a private garage.

A newspaper reprint, dated 1906, related that von Ersel died at the home of his friend, Joseph Luhr, in 1851, just two years after his arrival. Most surprising was that Governor Law of Maryland and professor Belke of Chicago were with him in Saint Marys when he died.

His valet, Gillis de Conver, joined the Benedictine Brothers in Saint Marystown and died in a railroad accident near the village.

The Industrial Revolution was not a revolution. It was but a phase in the evolution of Technology. There was no single event marking the starting date, but most of it occurred from 1820 to 1920.

Many of the early skirmishes in the in the Revolution took place in England where the railroad was developed and innovations in mining methods and iron production improved.

The low countries were quick to become participants but were both politically and socially unprepared for such innovation.

France adapted early but fell behind because of their own Revolution and the rise of Napoleon.

One of the events that spawned the Revolution was Colonel Drake's Titusville oil well in Elk County's back yard.

Riverboat man, train conductor, and speculator, **Colonel Drake** was born in 1819 and died impoverished in Bethlehem, PA in 1880.

Within weeks after Drake's success, fortune hunters poured into Venango County. The number of young men from Saint Marystown who went to seek their fortune in oil is not known.

The towns that sprung up along oil creek over the next decade were every bit as rough as Dawson, Abilene, White Horse, Dodge, and Cheyanne.

It is said that oil built the Erie Diocese.

Titusville Oil, a developing steel industry in Pittsburgh, and coal mining throughout the state made Pennsylvania the basic building block in the American phase of the industrial revolution.

Very soon the German colony in Elk County would get involved, for the railroad would soon arrive to Saint Marystown.

Plans began in the 1830s to construct a line connecting the Sunbury and Erie Railroads. Bank failures and other monetary problems delayed this proposed section between Lock Haven and Erie until well into the 1850s.

Notwithstanding a shortage of money, there were also a lack of roads, impenetrable forests, and recently discovered coal under the proposed railroad path.

On August 12, 1864, Chief Engineer, **Robert Fairies**, drove a final ceremonial spike which joined the Eastern and Western sections of the Sunbury & Erie Railroad. The location was the village of Tambine where Rt. 219 and Montmorenci Road intersect today. Work crews, trainmen and villagers were on hand to witness the event.

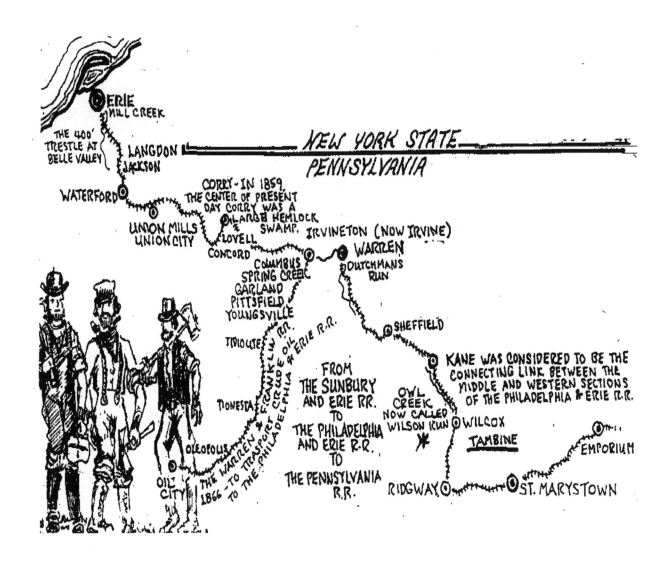

In the late 1850s, the first surveyors, land clearing teams, and land purchasing agents of the Sunbury and Erie Railroad would make their presence known in the Saint Marystown area.

Much of what we know derives from John Perkin's 1867 journal, put together during a trip from Erie to Philly for the Erie Dispatch Steam Printing Company.

The decade began with Irish Laborers and English overseers arriving to the settlement in 1860, and the colony would begin to shed its exclusive Bavarian Catholic Personality.

Although Saint Marys was settled to escape the anti-Catholic and anti- immigrant fever sweeping through the Eastern cities, the settlers did not take kindly to the Irish.

A generation or two later, the Irish would join with the Germans and force the first Slavs and from the sidewalks and onto the roads.

[*It was common to depict the Irishman as an ape*.]

In our own time some of the descendants of the early Irish have attempted to keep other "undesirables" out of their neighborhoods. Intolerance does seem always to be with us.

It was said that no Saint Marystown parents wanted a daughter to bring a son of the "old sod" home to meet the folks, but the Coleen's were perfectly acceptable.

Although the Irish were not greatly esteemed by most of the early Bavarians, they brought new blood, culture, and money to the colony which was what the commune would need to survive.

Irish laborers and their English Protestant bosses brough the English language and a need for more diverse religious services to the colony.

The German settlers were nothing if not practical, and *The Articles of the German Catholic Brotherhood* were fast becoming a passing curiosity.

Relating the story of Saint Marystown in the decade of the 1860s is a convoluted and complicated business. Although there is not much documentation, there were five important and intertwined factors to consider:

1.   The development of the railroad.
2.   The arrival of Irish immigrants.
3.   The introduction of Protestantism.
4.   The growth of local industry based on natural resources and the
       early coal and Timber empires.

By the end of the 1860s, St. Marys had parted ways with most aspects of its Bavarian Catholic Commune identity when the Saint Marys Parish Church began to conduct certain services in a language other than German, a practice that had been at the heart of dissention in the early settlers' Saint Alphonsus Parish in Baltimore.

In 1845, **Mrs. Alois Leffler** became the first Protestant to live in Saint Marystown.

Nineteen years later, **James Patton**, superintendent of the Saint Marys Coal Company, brought his Protestant family to Saint Marystown from Lycoming County, the first such family in the colony.

Patton frequently held prayer and hymn services in the company carpenter shop on Washington Road.

On July 8, 1866, the Reverend David Hull who was visiting Patton, preached the first protestant sermon in Saint Marystown.

Following the Franklin Pierce into the white house was **James Buchanan** (1856-1860), the only Pennsylvanian to hold the office and the sole Bachelor President to this day.

Buchanan was forced to move against the abolitionist, John Brown. Between Lincoln's election & inauguration, it was Buchanan who would determine the response to South Carolina's secession.

Although the Kansas Territory was in flames and Fort Sumpter beleaguered, Buchanan refused to recognize these events as acts of war.

He hoped for reconciliation and was determined to deliver an intact nation to President Elect, Abe Lincoln in 1861

Back in the little German speaking village of Saint Marystown, the Elk County Rifles were reorganized as the Elk Artillery Number 1, commanded by Captain C.H. Volk, a veteran of the Mexican War.

It numbered 50 men, most of whom were German born.

Immediately following South Carolina's secession, four months before the Declaration of war, Volk, in a personal letter to President Buchanan, wrote that the Elk Artillery (lacking cannons) were ready to fight to preserve the union at a day's notice.

The Elk Artillery was the third volunteer unit in the U.S. to offer their services to the President.

In 1858, the Lincoln-Douglas debates solidified the understanding that the back-woods lawyer was a defender of the Union and no friend of slavery.

The debates attracted the attention of the powerful Eastern Republicans.

LINCOLN, known as "The Railsplitter" by Congress, became the 16th President, winning an easy election in 1860, resulting from splits in both major parties.

He followed the policies of his predecessor regarding the seceded states until April 12, 1861, when General G.T. Beauregard ordered Confederate Artillery to fire on Fort Sumpter, igniting a war that Americans regarded as inevitable.

48 hours after Sumpter fell to the guns of the rebel states, Lincoln issued his call for 75,000 volunteers.

By the time the conflict ended, the dead bodies numbered nearly ten times that figure and at Gettysburg alone, more Americans would die than in all the previous wars combined.

S. Foster
1826-
1864.

We are coming, Father Abraham, three hundred thousand more,
From Mississippi's winding stream and from New England's shore.

We leave our plows and workshops, our wives and children dear,
With hearts too full for utterance, with but a silent tear.

We dare not look behind us but steadfastly before,
We are coming, Father Abraham, three hundred thousand more!

- James S. Gibbons/ music by Stephen Foster

Although President Buchanan did not call the Elk County Artillery to muster, and records from the period are scant, some research indicates that over one hundred men and boys from Saint Marystown answered President Lincoln's call to arms. Sixteen or more joined the 111 Pennsylvania Volunteers in Erie.

One hundred and nine men from Elk County became the Company G. "Wildcats" of the 42nd Pennsylvania Volunteers, the colorful *"Bucktails."*

The 74th, 84th and 105th, all had several Saint Marys men in their ranks, and at least seven Saint Marystown men served in the calvary.

Six or more gave the full measure.

When the Irish Railroaders came to Saint Marystown, the Abbot sent a young Bavarian born priest who was teaching at Saint Vincent to tend to the spiritual needs of the newcomers.

Later, **Father Emmeran Bliemel** would be assigned as Pastor for the Assumption Parish in Nashville Tennessee, and in 1863 the young Benedictine was permitted to join the 10th Tennessee Infantry.

Many of Bliemel's parishioners were members of this outfit, and they elected him chaplain.

He quickly earned a reputation for being in the thick of the fighting.

While making visits to wounded Confederate prisoners behind union lines, the Rebel Priest was suspected of spying. General W.S. Rosecrans wrote to his brother, Bishop Rosecrans of Saint Louis, that if pesky monk weren't recalled, he would be shot or hung.

So, the abbot called him back to Saint Vincent, but the message was either ignored or not delivered.

In late August 1864, the "Bloody" 10th Tennessee volunteers engaged William Sherman's men to halt the March to Atlanta.

1,500 rebel troops fell in the battle of Jonesboro, Georgia. When Bleimal's friend, Colonel W.M. Grace, Commander of the 10th, fell mortally wounded, Bleimal rushed to administer last rights and was killed in the act. He was only 32 years old.

Bleimal and Grace were buried near the battlefield.

He was the only Catholic Chaplain killed in the Civil War.

What follows are a few portraits of Saint Marystown men involved in the war between the states. They were randomly selected, for every veteran's story is of interest.

Harry Williams GAR – US Lot 150 Presbyterian Cemetery Williams served as Sergeant for Company G of the 2nd New York rifles and later joined the Navy. He worked as a Railroad Engineer and after the war was murdered in Saint Marys in 1883.

Captain William Kopp served as Lieutenant in the German Army and a Captain under Hancock in the Civil War. Kopp Fought through Gettysburg, Bull Run and Antietam. He was a stone cutter and worked on the old monastery, courthouse and "English Church."

Charles Bayer was pressed into the Confederate Army for 7 months while working in Texas. He escaped and joined the Federal forces. He then built "Ironclads" in Cairo, Illinois.

After the war, he opened Bayer furniture in St. Marys.

Charles Herbstritt answered the call and was wounded on Cemetery Hill at Gettysburg and died of smallpox.

Peter Herbstritt fought at Bentonville, S.C., and was present for Joe Johnson's surrender.

Martin lied about his age and fought at Saylor's Creek. He was present at Lee's surrender.

Drummer Boy Jessie Varner joined the "Bucktails" on the first call and fought through the war, being wounded seven times.

He hung himself in his barn in 1897 when he was no longer able to do farm work.

Henry Biglan, Company K, PA Mounted Volunteer, fought in the Calvary action on the 1st day of Gettysburg and later rode as a runner between Meade & Hancock.

He was on guard duty in Washington when Lincoln was shot. His daughter married D.J. Driscoll.

Mallison, **F.X. Beberger, Andrew Dippold, Mike Huff, George Kingsley, Jake Schubert, Lt George Smith,** and **Tom Zimmitt** were all members of the hard fighting 111th PA Volunteers and saw action at 2nd Bull Run, Chancellorsville, Antietam, Gettysburg, Lookout Mountain and Sherman's march.

Jacob Malison
(Born in England 1841)

F.X. Sosenheimer, a bugler, enlisted at 16 and was with the 12th Calvalry. He opened a plumbing and tinners' shop on Market Street. Today, the Fleming and Hanes business is a direct descendent of his shop.

Thomas Kane (1822-1880) descended from Mayflower Puritans and Revolutionary War heroes. He and his brother, **Elisha**, differed early with the rest of the family on the slavery issue.

Educated in Paris, he fought with the young radical partisans on the barricades. When he returned to America, he became a director in the Underground Railroad, later accepting a special assignment to Utah where he was instrumental in preventing the frontier war and winning the undying gratitude of many Mormons.

He founded the town of Kane and was the 1st Pennsylvanian to offer his services to Governor Curtain.

When he raised his famous 13th PA Reserves, he was living in Jones Township.

Answering Curtain's famous call for infantry and marksmen, Tom Kane began enlisting troops in Elk and McKean counties.

109 men and boys were likely borrowed from the lumber camps around Ridgway and Saint Marystown.

201

The famous emblem was adopted when McKean County recruit, **Jim Lundgren**, cut the tail from a deer hide hanging outside a Smethport near Kane's headquarters. He put it on his hat and thus created the "Bucktails."

His recruits gathered at Driftwood where 315 men and Kane's horse (called, Bob, by most of the men) floated on four large lumberman's rafts for on April 27th.

They debarked down the Sinnemahoning and into history. The men paid for the raft wood out of their own pockets.

Often on the journey, the Bucktails were forced to jump into the cold rapids to free the large rafts trapped on rocks.

Men from Saint Marystown who are known to have been with the Bucktails include:

Captain L. Gifford, Theophilus Devoge, Reuben Keller, Joseph Hoffman (killed at Spotsylvania), Sharpshooter **William Knecht (Knight)** and **Jesse Varner** – the Drummer boy.

By the early 1860s, people living in Saint Marystown countryside began to mine coal. The names of the original owners of the Saint Marys Coal Company seem to have been lost to history. The 36-inch vein opened in September 1863 and July 1864. The aforementioned James Patton was the superintendent.

The Saint Marys Coal Company was the colony's first big business. It employed many men and boys. The Coal Company also built the first company houses in Saint Marystown. Most of them have been remodeled and still stand on Washington Street. The Saint Marys Coal Company mines, numbered 10, 11, and 12, were located on either side of the Washington Road.

A tramway known as the Coal Chutes was erected over the Sunbury and Erie trackage shortly after the railway was completed. Coal could then be loaded directly into railroad hoppers from the big wooden structure.

The "Chutes" connected the mines on Bunker Hill and on the present-day Beagle Club land. They crossed Washington Road, the Elk Creek, and eventually the Shawmut tracks and burned in 1906 along with the newer nearby P.R.R. Tipple.

The "Chutes"

John Coryell had a varied and successful business career before becoming treasurer of the coal company in 1866.

The same year **Dr. Eben J. Russ** became the company physician.

Although neither of these men were originally stockholders in the mines, some generally associate them with the Saint Mary's Coal Company.

They grew up in the Williamsport area.

Together, they founded the Coryell and Russ General Merchandise Company.

Coryell never lived in Saint Marys but spent much time in the town.

Russ practiced medicine in St. Marys and created a structure which would would become the first library and later the Towne House.

Not a lot is recorded about the town's early coal mines. Besides the Saint Marys Coal Company operation, the Eldridge Coal Company was another of the early concerns, mining approximately 180 tons of coal a day. The openings were on the east slopes of the hill above Silver Creek.

The remains of the old trestle and "boney" pikes could still be found near the shooting range and priests' canal in the 1940s.

Early mining methods were primitive wheelbarrow operations.

Coal mining in the area did not reach its peak until World War I and declined sharply afterwards.

"Uncle John" Coryall and Dr. Russ are largely remembered for their philanthropic contributions to the community, but what should be remembered is that the wealth of the company mines was accumulated partially through the labors of dozens of boys between ten and fourteen who worked 12 to 15 hours a day without holidays off or any safety regulations.

Accidents in the mines were frequent and often fatal or crippling. There was no workman's compensation, and an incapacitated worker became a family burden.

Rarely was a miner paid in currency. Instead, the worker was remunerated with company store credits, which were rarely enough to clear his debt to the store. When one bought clothes or tools or food anywhere but the store, that one often was terminated from the company.

An story relates that Dr. Eben Russ, upon discovering that a miner had used a Canadian coin to pay for a pick in the Company Store, traveled several miles that night to receive payment in "good" money.

The Redemptorists erected a sawmill in the earliest days of the colony which initiated the building of the wood structures in Saint Marystown.

Unlike other country villages, St. Marystown had no waterway. So, although it could produce sawn lumber for its own use, it was unable to market the forest product.

Many young Saint Marystown men worked in neighboring log operations. Some became members of the legendary Raftsmen of the Clarion River, but logging would not become a major St. Marys Industry until the advent of the railroad.

Although the priest's sawmill had made lumber available from the early days of the colony, in the 1860s there was still much broad axe and hand adz work in Saint Marystown, some of which is still visible in old farmhouses and barns.

Broad brimmed hats were worn by the pitmen to keep the sawdust out of their eyes and inside their clothing.

Although any traces of the old saw pits have disappeared from the Saint Marys area, we can be certain that much of the early lumber used in the colony was obtained an exhausting means.

The Robel Sawmill (1850s) was the first of the smaller family sawmills. It was acquired and enlarged in 1858 by a young Prussian immigrant, **John B. Niemoller** (Neimiller).

The location later became famous and known as "Zwack's" pond.

John Kaul, a Bavarian, arrived at the settlement in 1844, having walked from Buffalo.

He then built a log cabin on Saint Michael Street. The same year, he was married to Kunnigunda Brindle by one of the Redemptorists. The marriage had been arranged in Bavaria.

A few years later, Kaul farmed a tract of uncleared land on Brusselles Road and had eight children, Andrew Joseph (who died in infancy) Kate (Lanzel), John, Kunnegunda (Kronenwetter), Catherine (Windfelder), Mary, and Joseph.

John Kaul
1814-1877

Andrew Kaul left his father's farm and took up lumberjacking in 1862.

Over the next five years, he would work on many lumbering and bark contracts and engage in numerous partnerships with veteran loggers and jobbers.

In 1866, he contracted in the West Creek Road area and in 1868 returned to the Saint Marystown area to purchase the Pine Stands from Benzinger, Eschbach and others

.

Later that year, he built a sawmill near the headwater of iron run. The mill operated for eight years.

Thereafter the equipment was moved to Kaul's new summit mill near the location of the Elk County Home on West Creek Road.

Andrew Kaul (1845-1905) now joins Czvikowicz, Sabastian Wimmer, Jacob Schaut, Ignatius Garner, Mattius Benzinger and John Eschbach in the pantheon of the Men who made Saint Marys.

There will be little that will go on in the growing Elk County village over the next 70 years that will not bear the stamp of this early Bavarian farmer, woodsman, and entrepreneur.

On April 15th, 1865, just six days after Lee Handed Grant his sword at Appomattox Court House, Lincoln was shot in the young nation's first act of regicide.

"Honest Abe," considered by many to have been the most dictatorial of the American Presidents was never popular, but following his martyrdom, he was sanitized, lionized, and beatified.

Today, he is considered to have been an astute politician, a superb judge of character, a philosopher, a manic depressive, and a backwoodsman who was steadfastly intent on preserving the Union.

Lincoln is rivaled only George Washington for the honor of having been our GREATEST PRESIDENT AND AMERICAN.

Several coaches painted black carried Lincoln home again. There was a strange silence along the railroad track as nobody spoke when it passed.

211

From the LONESOME TRACK:

A LONESOME TRAIN ON A LONESOME TRACK
SEVEN COACHES PAINTED BLACK
A SMALL TRAIN, A QUIET TRAIN
CARRYING MR. LINCOLN HOME AGAIN...

LINCOLN SAID, "WHAT'S BEEN BOTHERIN' ME
IS HOW TO MAKE THE WAR AND WORD AGREE..."

IT WAS A STRANGE A QUIET CROWD,
NOBODY WANTED TO TALK OUT LOUD...

YOU COULD HEAR THAT WHISTLE FOR MILES AROUND
CRYING FREEEEEEDOM! ...

FREEDOM IS A THING THAT HAS NO ENDING
IT NEEDS TO BE CARED FOR – IT NEEDS DEFENDING...

THEY WERE HIS PEOPLE. HE WAS THEIR MAN,
YOU COULDN'T TELL WHERE LINCOLN LEFT OFF AND THE PEOPLE BEGAN.

On August 15, 1864, the first locomotive rolled through Saint Marystown bringing with it the outside world.

The railroad would deal a mortal blow to the old "wagon wheel" plan for the colony layout and would also serve as the village nucleus for the next 100 years.

Houses were often built with their front door facing the tracks.

The last example is the former Rebic home, which became the Elk Baptist Church at 1039 Brusselles Street.

Stores and business were quick to locate close to what would become the hub of village activity.

213

Erie Avenue, Mill, Depot and Railroad streets became the commercial centers of Saint Marystown.

Dairymen, timber contractors, fur trappers, coal mine & sawmill owners suddenly had the means to sell their wares to more than just those living in or near Saint Marystown.

The railroad allowed direct access to the Great Lake ports and the large coastal cities to the east. There was a time when eleven or more trains a day would chug through the village.

With the trains came smooth-talking drummers, peddlers from the big towns and salesmen of every kind. Manufactured goods previously impossible to obtain were made available.

Even fresh seafood arrived in Saint Marys daily.

Previously, there was little reason for salesman to pay a visit the near destitute colony in 1860, but the Railroad changed all that.

Many of the early hotels were temporary rooming houses for new settlers, for examplem the Luhr House on Center Street the Wellendorf on Saint Marys Street.

Others were roadside taverns and stagecoach stop-overs, such as Stebich's on Fehrenbach Hill, the Inn at Pumpkin Hill in Glenn Hazel, and the White Pine Hotel on the Centreville Pike.

THE ALPINE HOUSE, ABOUT 1868.

The Alpine house stood on Railroad Street (now Erie Avenue) in 1876 and was followed by the Wachtel House which burned in the fire of 1880. Later, the Commercial Hotel, which became the Mullendean, occupied the approximate location. In the mid-1860s, the Presbyterians held Sunday services in the Alpine House.

The Sunbury and Erie Railroad soon became the Philadelphia and Erie, hence the name "Erie Avenue." The first of the railroad hotels also took the name of the railroad line. The Philadelphia was later to be known as the Franklin Hotel.

We left the Benedictine Sisters in the beat-up
Redemptorist building, a two-room cabin with
a single door and a sagging roof.

The school was in the same condition.

After the strong-willed Mother Benedicta Reipp
departed, **Sister M. Theresa Vogel** took over the prioress position for 18 years
(1857-1875).

She was elected again from 1878 until 1881 and can be considered the builder of
the Saint Joseph Motherhouse.

Despite the extreme poverty and hardship endured by the first Benedictine Sisters,
twelve girls from the Colony sought admission to the order of 1852. The same year

three more sisters and two postulants arrived from the Saint Walburga Mother Convent in Eichstadt, Germany.

By 1855, Saint Walburga had contributed thirteen sisters to the Saint Marystown Convent, which then had 39 members.

As more local girls joined the sisterhood, the cabin was enlarged by the addition of a one-story wing, allowing young girls to board.

The sisters also taught boys and would serve as public-school teachers from 1855 until 1895.

With the mushrooming growth of the Saint Marystown Sisterhood, it became apparent that a larger convent was needed. Land was then granted to the sisters at the rear of the new church and $3,500.00 was raised through the influence of Abbot Wimmer, the King Louis Mission Society, and Reverend Father Miller, Court Chaplain.

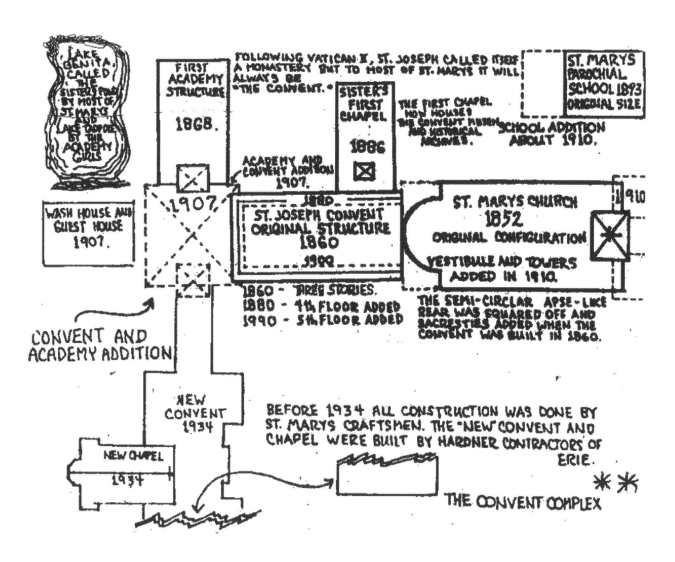

In 1860, the 45' by 80' two-story structure was erected. Father Agedius Christoff was Prior at the time and served as the architect, building supervisor and paymaster.

Frequently, the cash ran out as there was little in the colony.

In the face of adversity, the nuns were still able to wish one another "Fröhliche Weihnachten," on Christmas Day in their own building.

Still faintly visible in the curved wall was the high alter in the Saint Marys Church.

It is possible to make out the outline of the openings, through which the sisters could attend Mass without leaving the Convent confines. They also gathered for night and dawn prayers.

By 1856, four sisters from Saint Joseph's in Saint Marys - at the request of Father Hartmann of Erie - founded Saint Benedict's. Their intention was to teach the children of German immigrants.

Such would be the first of dozens of outgrowths which could trace their origins to the Motherhouse in Saint Marystown.

Some aspects of what would become the highly regarded and fully accredited Saint Benedict's Academy for girls were present almost as long as the sisters themselves.

There were girls of both elementary and secondary grade levels boarding with the nuns even before they left the rundown Redemptorist complex.

Eight years after the convent was erected a large academy building was put up at a right angle to the church and convent (1868).

Brother Wilhelm Lechner, known affectionately in the colony as Brother William, played a major role in the construction.

Of the 15 rooms in the new three-story academy building, originally the 2nd and 3rd floors were both contained just one long room.

In the years that followed hundreds of girls attended the Academy as day students.

Most of these matriculated from nearby communities of eastern states but were soon accompanied by students from the far west, the Caribbean and even Scandinavia.

All boarders were required to write home monthly.

A typical sophomore curriculum would include Christian doctrine, Church History, Physical Science, Political Geography, English Composition, Latin, German, French, Physiology, Hygiene, Civics, Book-Keeping, Arithmetic, Algebra, Botany, Drawing, Sewing and Music.

The cost per semester including room and board = $80.00.

The story of the first Protestant congregation in Saint Marystown is one of adversity, dedication, and faith. The presence of the new sect in the village implied a cultural antagonism for the Colony Charter which stated: "People of the same faith, the same language, the same manners and customs," meaning Bavarian Catholics only.

When the Presbyterians opted to build their Church, there were but 20 members in the congregation with little money and many setbacks. The first sermon was preached in the unfinished church in March 1869. It was dedicated in 1870.

Carpenters were summoned from Williamsport to erect a two-story frame structure, and work progressed slowly.

At the time of this writing, the old building is still giving yeoman's service on Grant Street as an Apartment house.

The town got a bank in 1867. It was called The Saint Mary's Bank.

The original stockholders included W.M. Singerly, Sampson Short, Louis Vollmer, John G. Hall, and J.K.P. Hall.

The bank had a capital stock of $30,000.00. It was located where the CMF now stands. No picture of it is known to exist.

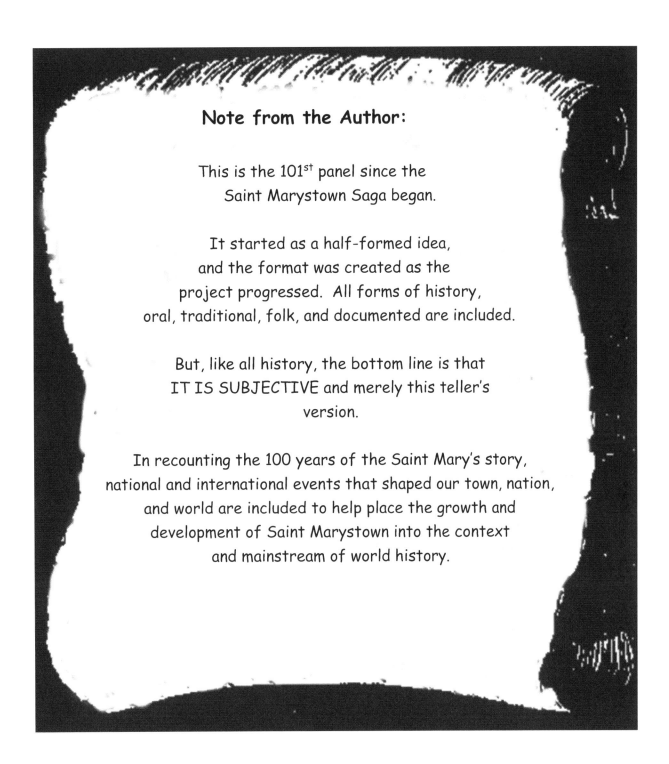

Note from the Author:

This is the 101st panel since the
Saint Marystown Saga began.

It started as a half-formed idea,
and the format was created as the
project progressed. All forms of history,
oral, traditional, folk, and documented are included.

But, like all history, the bottom line is that
IT IS SUBJECTIVE and merely this teller's
version.

In recounting the 100 years of the Saint Mary's story,
national and international events that shaped our town, nation,
and world are included to help place the growth and
development of Saint Marystown into the context
and mainstream of world history.

The **17ᵗʰ U.S. President, Andrew Johnson,** assumed the volatile task of Reconstruction after the assassination of Lincoln.

Johnson, who was formerly Lincoln's appointed Military Governor of Tennessee, followed his predecessor's policy of leniency for the defeated South, which resulted in his being our first impeached president.

His office was saved by a single vote in the Senate. It is of interest to note that while Lincoln was a Republican, Vice President Johnson was a Democrat.

Johnson's presidency is usually remembered by the impeachment hearings, but it is important to also recognize that 13ᵗʰ Amendment abolishing slavery and the 14ᵗʰ granting citizenship to former slaves were both ratified during Johnson's term.

The vast Alaska territory was also acquired in 1867 when Russia, fearing British expansion peddled it off for $7,200,000 or two cents and acre. Much of the nation thought it a waste of money.

As this most important decade ended, Ulysses S. Grant occupied the White House. Johnson had hoped to have been nominated by his party, but **Horatio Seymour** was chosen and then defeated by the Republican Civil War Hero, U.S. Grant.

President Grant enjoyed trout fishing in Elk County, and a special railway siding was laid to accommodate his railway coach, hence the little hamlet of Grant in Benezette Township.

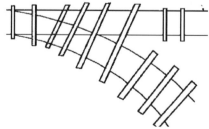

Grant's name can be found in the Medix Hotel Guest Book.

In the mid-1860s, **R.C. McGill** (1818-1901) came to Saint Marystown.

Although he was a prominent businessman, pillar of the church and community leader, he remains a mysterious figure. He was always called, General, but a search of the many volumes of Pennsylvania Volunteers reveals no such general in any Army branch.

McGill was born in Ireland circa 1818. Neither his wife Lydia's maiden nor his first name appears his in his wife's obituaries.

General
R.C. McGill
(1818-1801)

He seems always to have been known as General R.C. and even his tombstone is so marked. It is only by reading his will that we discover his name was Rodger. He held the rank of Captain in Huntingdon Guard, a county militia.

He appears to have been hurt in a training accident and discharged shortly afterwards. He built his mill in 1865.

McGill had built two Grist Mills in Huntingdon prior to coming to Saint Marys. Mill Street took its name from this landmark.

McGill's (later Ritter's) Mill was built on the site of an early small mill, owned by John Steffen.

Of the many Saint Marystown mills, McGill's was the most successful and longest running.

An 1870 Saint Marystown map depicts the mill whose foundry was located where the former Modern Dairy stood. His broom factory was situated on Mill Street. His home was the only building on McGill Street at the time.

Sister Evangelist McGill O.S.B.

Sister Benedict McGill O.S.B.

Sister Philomena McGill, O.S.B.

The McGill's had seven children, and three of their four daughters became nuns. R.C. McGill died in Allegheny, Pennsylvania, where he had retired for his health but is buried in the Saint Mary's Cemetery.

In 1877, the floor of the new Catholic Church, near the McGill home, was discovered to be on fire. General McGill severely burned his hands fighting the blaze.

LOUIS RIEL, (1844-1885)

With the Civil War raging in the states, many candidates began to fear American territorial expansion. A dominion formed in 1867, uniting Quebec, Ontario, Nova Scotia, and New Brunswick. The other provinces followed suit over the next few years.

The union brought about the breakup of the vast Rupert's land territories, occupied chiefly by **Métis,** people of mixed and Indian blood, most of whom were descendants of the Hudson Bay fur trappers. The division resulted in the Red River and Northwest rebellions led by the fiery Métis, **Louis Riel**.

Fearing they would lose their lands to new settlers, the Métis openly revolted. After the effort was crushed, lands were set aside for the Métis, and Riel was elected to the House of Commons. He was pardoned but refused the seat he had won.

After becoming an American citizen and spending time in asylums, Riel returned to the Métis, this time in Saskatchewan, to assist his people to hold their territory.

In 1885, he was captured and hung. His martyrdom remains one of the division points between English and French Canadians.

Great political activity took place in the nations bordering the states both to the north and the south in the late 1860

Benito Juarez, an Indian reformer who when Governor of Oaxaca enacted laws reducing the powers of the church and military, was elected President of Mexico.

Because of a financial crisis, he then suspended payment on all Europeans loans for two years.

As the U.S. was engaged in a Civil War, **Louis Napoleon** felt free to invade Mexico and establish a French presence in North America. In 1964, he crowned his crony, **Maximillian**, the Archduke of Austria, emperor of Mexico.

BENITO JUÁREZ (1806 - 1872)

It was Juarez who led his country in their effort against the French invaders up to the time when America's war ended, and the northern neighbor could enforce the Monroe Doctrine.

When the French forces were repulsed, Maximillian was capture and executed.

Juarez is Mexico's Washington, Jefferson, and Lincoln. He was consistent in his integrity, concern for the poor, and efforts for political and social reforms.

His three terms in office were unprecedented south of the border.

There seems to have been little or no notice of the village's 25th anniversary. Saint Marystown was still small, poor, and underpopulated. Its survival was precarious, but the railroad and the infant coal and lumber business were changing things. The town had a lot going for it but no time to attend to its 25th year anniversary.

We'll now look at a few of the most important figures involved in the colony founding a quarter century later:

FATHER ALEXANDER CZVIKOWICZ, was living in Louisiana and doing heroic work with victims of the yellow fever, utilizing his fluency in seven languages to bring honor to himself and his order.

In 1867, the inexhaustible Ignatius Garner had been elected first Burgess, first postmaster, first Church organist and nearly everything else. He would soon organize the first band, fire company and build a foundry. Because of his community dedication, relations between him, Eschbach, and Benzinger were strained.

His old friend, Jacob Schaut, married his sister Magdalena. After several trips to Bavaria to recruit settlers, Schaut settled down to raise a family and pursue his woodworking trade..

By 1867 Benzinger remained one of Baltimore's most prominent citizens but was ailing and not too active.

Not much has been discovered about John Eschbach, the enigmatic Baltimore contractor. He does not appear to have ever visited Saint Marys and was still doing contract work in 1867.

Von Schroeder had again hit the skids and was drifting between monasteries painting portraits for his bread and bed.

The energetic Father Boniface Wimmer, still a staunch supporter of Saint Marystown, continued as Archabbot for another 20 years.

King Ludwig's liaison with Lola Montez had resulted in his abdication.

Several short-lived industries operated in the Saint Marystown area in the 1860s and 1870s. Among them were the Schultz Tannery on Saint Marys Street.

In the swampy eastern section of the village, known as "Frog Hollow" (present day Fourth Street), a small brickyard was established.

In 1873, the brickyard was operated by a Mr. Walker and a Mr. Hoffman.

Soft red bricks were made from Elk Creek clay, and some are still to be found in St. Marys buildings.

The Girl Scout (Proctor House) is one of these.

233

Besoms, as early brooms were called, were usually made of birch twigs tied around an ash handle with willow.

As flooring modernized, a more efficient besom was needed, and broomcorn was grown for the purpose.

Of the several broom factories in early Saint Marystown, General McGill's Mill Street operation is the best known.

It was in the late 1860s and early 1870s that the first of a dozen or so cigar factories opened downtown.

Local girls were employed to roll cigars for gentlemen.

Although the Industrial Revolution was beginning to change the way people lived and worked in post-Civil War America, prospering towns were dependent on certain businesses. Among the most important were the mills, particularly grist mills, sawmills, and foundries.

Ignatius Garner & Sons, the Kaul's and McGill all owned early Saint Marystown foundries.

Many farms, wagon makers, and livery stables contained their own small blacksmith shops.

Railroads, sawmills, and other developing industries relied on blacksmith shops to cast iron, brass, bronze, wet sand, mold, and machine metal.

The largest and longest lived of the foundries was the Stackpole Street Elk Engineering works (1904-1963)

In 1871 the Benedictine Gristmill on Elk Creek below the Old Redemptorist complex burned for the second time. Not much is known about these fires, except that the village had not yet organized a fire department.

The citizens of the town fought fire with an inefficient bucket brigade and nothing more.

By the time the priest's mill burned for the second time, the village had other grist mills.

Shortly after the Civil War, George Schmidt, a 2nd Lieutenant in the Union Army was granted land in the present-day Silver Creek area. He built a sawmill a sawmill and few years later moved his operation to the Fourth/Washington Street intersection. The enterprise would change hands and become the Schaut Planning Mill and Building Supplies.

Life expectancy in the 1860s-1870s was often no more than 45 years. Many women died in childbirth, and men were often killed or maimed in horrible accidents. Widows and widowers usually remarried because life without a helpmate was exceedingly difficult in early frontier America.

Death was common, and burial was quick and simple. There were upwards of 14 graveyards in the village of Saint Marystown.

Railroads were especially onerous. Hardly a week would pass without a decapitation or a hacked off limb. Conductors and trainmen would often fall between cars or were caught by couplers. Hobos were also killed while walking along the tracks or hopping freights.

Children too were killed as they played on the tracks, and horses pulling buggies often ran into trains at crossings.

14 YEAR OLD OLIVER TWILLINGER, WORKING WITH HIS FATHER SAWING LATHING AT KAUL'S SUMMIT MILL CAUGHT HIS SLEEVE AND WAS PULLED INTO THREE WHIRRING SAW BLADES. MAY, 1877.

Logging camps and mills were also dangerous work environments. Deadfalls, axe accidents, and loose logs at log chutes killed many men as did exposed saw blades, flapping belts, and unguarded moving machinery in the mills. There were many such mishaps, and they were often rather gruesome. Mine and farm mishaps also accounted for many deaths.

Hot water tanks had yet to be invented so when needed, water was heated on the stove or hearth. Such water was used for cooking, cleaning, washing clothes and bathing.

Many young children were scalded when their parents stumbled while carrying boiling water.

Drownings at wells and watering troughs were common too.

The Elk Creek was an apple of discord in Saint Marystown. The stream which served the settler's initial water supply became littered with trash, swollen with sewage, and polluted with highly acidic sawmill runoff. Putrefying tannery waste and later toxic carbon residue were also discharged to the creek.

In the 1870s, pressure from the village resulted in the construction of South Saint Marys and Market Street bridges.

Reporters wrote of the Creek's toxic effluence and suggested that the state of the water's quality might just have been the source of the frequent outbreaks of Diphtheria and Scarlet Fever.

In March 1876, A Miller family living in Benzinger Township lost five of six children to Scarlet Fever in the course of two weeks.

In June 1882, an eight-year-old son of Mr. & Mrs. L.C. Bayer also died from the Scarlet Fever. He was the fourth child lost in as many weeks.

Such tragedies were not uncommon.

By October 1881, ninety-three souls had been buried in the Saint Marystown Cemetery. Seventy of these were children, and of those, forty-nine had died of Diphtheria, literally suffocating while their parents helplessly watched.

Such epidemics were a yearly event before 1900.

The logic in December 1878 was to have the colonists gargle and swallow a dram of kerosene as a Diphtheria preventative.

In November 1886, parents were told to gargle and ingest mixtures of sulfur three times a day to prevent the spread of the dreaded ailment.

Typhoid, whooping cough, edema, and consumption were the catalyst for the demise of many of the early Settlers.

Nuns on the streets of Saint Marystown were everyday sights during the first half of the 1900s, as they could be seen walking to and from the convent, schools, and hospital. Earlier in the 1860s, 70s, and 80s, Benedictine postulants were also common village sights.

Most of their names and stories are lost to us as the early historians kept few records of them.

Some surviving names at the time of this writing include: **Brothers Giles, Karo, Pius, William, Bruno, and Karl Wilhelm**.

We don't how many were the sons of Saint Marystown settlers, but by 1870, there were forty brothers living in the colony.

These men, often rough and uneducated, were blacksmiths, cooks, herdsmen, carpenters, bakers, millers, stone cutters, wood carvers, teachers, horticulturalists, brick layers, glass blowers, and smiths of every kind.

They were in many ways the original village craftsmen, and their story is an unwritten chapter of Saint Marystown that warrants further research.

At Saint Vincent Abbey in Latrobe in 1886, the inexhaustible Abbot Wimmer noticed the consequential supply of young Saint Marystown men studying Holy Orders and founded a seminary school and monastery in the Bavarian Catholic settlement in Elk County.

Prior **Paulinius Wenkman**, a prodigious Benedictine builder, who had arrived at Saint Marystown in 1866, was assigned the project. The Benedictine Brothers would provide the bulk of the labor.

The nearly four-storied structure was constructed near the ramshackle Redemptorist complex, which it seems was still occupied by the Benedictine monks. The Grandiose plans called for the building to be known as Saint Gregory's College.

Construction began in 1870.

Although Saint Gregory's never came to pass, the stone building did serve as a monastery for the priests and brothers for close to 20 years.

TRIVIA: An old stone bench to the right of the hospital once faced the monastery entrance. The monks built it from leftovers.

It was a favorite trysting place for young men courting the Pilz girls who lived in the monastery after the departure of Benedictines.

My [the writer's] Grandmother was one of them.

The monastery was just one of the relevant buildings to be erected in the late 1800s.

In 1870, Saint Marystown assembled a Town Hall on Market Street which also served as council chamber, jail, band room and first library.

The Irish gained a parish and their own Sacred Heart Church on Center Street in 1876.

It would come to be known as the "English Church," as opposed to the "German" church just up the hill.

Boys and girls also scored a brick public school on the Maurus/Church Street corner in 1875. It was situated close to the convent which supplied most of the teachers in those years.

The Philadelphia & Erie Railroad locomotives secured a roundhouse in the late 1870s. It stood near to the point where Depot Street became Curry Avenue. At the time, there were two Charles Streets in Saint Marystown. Curry Ave was named at the Post Office's insistence on a differentiation.

Of the many famous and notable people who have resided in Saint Marystown, few were more notable than the famous engineer, **Sabastian Wimmer** (1831-1921).

Wimmer was born in Ratisbon, Bavaria, receiving his engineering degree in Munich.

In 1851 he arrived in America just six years after his uncle, the Reverend Abbot Boniface Wimmer, who founded Saint Vincent.

His career began as a city engineer in Pittsburgh where he established himself as one of the nation's foremost railroad engineers, later working in New Orleans and being appointed assistant engineer of the Minneapolis & Cedar Valley Railroad.

He then joined the Pennsylvania Railroad Engineering Corps and attempted to join the G.A.R. Engineers during the Civil War but was considered too valuable as a civilian.

He went on to work on the Wabash Railroad, the Pittsburgh & Erie, the New York City and the Northern and the P.S.S.N., the logging railroad of John DuBois.

Wimmer's fame derived from planning and building a railroad viaduct which connected a railroad to Mexico City, a feat many other engineers had tried and failed.

The trestles he erected over the dry lakebed surrounding the city still bear his name. Wimmer was friend of the Emperor Maximillian at the time.

Wimmer married Lavina Blakely, the daughter of a Pittsburgh alderman in 1857, raising four sons in Saint Marystown. Lavina's brother, John, also found his way to Saint Marystown and opened a store on Center Street.

Although Wimmer was often away, he voted in every election and is buried in Saint Marys.

He built a large home on North Saint Michael Street (now 119 Maurus Street) and served three terms in the State House where he attempted to move the Elk County Seat to Saint Marystown. During the last two years of his life, he became Saint Vincent's first postmaster at the age of 90.

Sixty-five of Wimmer's diaries are stored in the archives of the Saint Marys-Benzinger Township Historical Society.

Mr. & Mrs. Walmesley lived in the colony in the 1870s. They were Protestants but joined the Catholic Church after their son, who died studying for the priesthood at Saint Vincent, became the colony's first convert. For many years, George Walmesely was the only Republican in Saint Marystown, and it would be 1942 before the first Republican was elected mayor.

J.K.P. Hall, who became the partner of Andrew Kaul, had a law office on South Saint Marys Street. He was an early organizer of Saint Marys Baseball.

John Salter served two years in the Union Army and returned home to invent a repeating rifle, shotgun, and mine car brake.

He was the best known of several Saint Marystown gunsmiths.

Joseph Winfelder married a daughter of early Saint Marystown merchant, George Weis. He was a brewer, saloon keeper, Saint Marystown Mayor and County Treasurer. His old homestead was torn down when Elk Towers was built.

Charles Luhr, store, hotel keeper, brewer, mayor, councilman, justice of the peace associate judge and member of the Pennsylvania State Legislature.

Professor Frederick Be(a)rnhart(d) was the Saint Marystown Choirmaster and violin/piana/organ teacher. He composed a mass performed on Easter in 1884. In early documents, his name appears with E, A, D and T.

"The Old Priest", Father Erhardus Vanino, son of a Bavarian Army Officer Vanino said his first mass in Saint Marystown. He spent most of his priestly life in the saddle ministering in the Elk & Shippen areas.

Unfortunately, Captain **Charles H. Volk** is another of those important early local figures of which little is known. We do know that he served in the Mexican War, likely as a commissioned officer.

We do not know that he married or what brought him to Saint Marystown, but in 1860 he was commander of the Saint Marystown militia (1st Elk Artillery).

Under him, they became the 3rd unit to offer immediate services to President Buchannan upon South Carolina's secession.

Although the president did not take up the offer of these patriotic men, Volk served four years in the G.A.R. as an infantry officer with the '84th Pennsylvania Volunteers.

Upon returning to his adopted home, Volk built a hotel-tavern-Brewery, known as Captain Volk's Lager and Eating Saloon. When his health was failing, he sold the downtown establishment to Lawrence Vogel.

Accounts vary, but it might be that the Captain purchased the Sorg Farm overlooking the village from the South and the site of a clean spring. Volk called the countryside Brewery he established, the Benzinger Spring Brewery.
It is time for **Peter Straub** to enter the Saint Marystown story.

In 1933, Frank Volk, 83, a railroad engineer from Santa Monica, California, visited the editor of the Saint Marystown newspaper.

Windfelder & Volk's Brewmaster, Peter Straub, of Wurtemburg, Germany (1850-1912)

It was his third visit in the sixty years since leaving Saint Marystown, and nothing is known of his conversations.

Were we to accept oral accounts, there might have been as many as eight breweries in Saint Marystown which pre-date the Straub and St. Marys Breweries.

1.   Michael "Beer" Hartz Brewery on North Michael Street
2.   Windfelder (later Luhr) near present day American Legion
3.   Babel (Marquardt) - Cross Road
4.   Mountain Brewery – Top of North Michael Street owned successively by Burgess Wesnitzer, W.M. Gies, Charles Walker and Conrad Marquardt
5.   Dorner – Center Street, near the Church Street intersection
6.   Wittman – Corner of Brusselles Street and South Saint Michael Street
7.   Captain Volk – Erie Avenue, site of Present-Day Moose Club
8.   Carl Klausman – Railroad Street

Peter Straub purchased Volk's countryside brewery in 1878. From that time, Straub beer became The St. Marys Beer. No coal, lumber, refractory, carbon or would symbolize Saint Marys as did the brown, foaming beverage brewed from the pure crystal water of the Sorg Farm spring.

[Peter Straub was originally a cooper (barrel maker). Millions of barrels were needed in both Europe and American in the 19th century.

When Straub died, the brewery's duties were assumed by his son, Tony. The establishment was then re-named "Peter Straub's Son's Brewery" and remains as one of the last family-owned breweries in the United States. It was said to be the largest of the small breweries and the smallest of the large.

Although the brewery was not cited for bootlegging during prohibition, it was rumored that on the day when the 18th Amendment was repealed, the brewery was in full production of Straub's "High Test."

But that's another story.

In the pioneer homesteads of our Saint Marystown forbearers, beer was a staple at many family meals. During the Great Depression, many children were fed hard bread and warm beer. They called it "beer soup."

The marriage between Saint Marystown and beer has been denounced and criticized, but such has been a cultural attribute since the village's earliest years and seems likely to remain so.

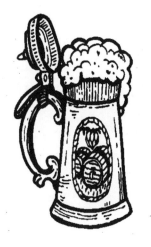

A seemingly unending fire alarm rang across the 19ᵗʰ century rural America when candles, open hearths, kerosene lamps, uncured hay and/or lightning all did their bit in making fire an ever-present foe in the wooden villages and countryside.

In Saint Marystown, as in most villages, numerous homes and barns were lost.

Both Rogan's Railway Hotel and The Alpine House burned in the years we are now visiting.

The Kaul structures were especially susceptible to large fires.

Andy's home was destroyed in 1876, and his Summit Sawmill was taken by flames in 1879.

In 1887, John Kaul's foundry and machine shop had also burned.

Following the fire, the house that Andrew Kaul built in 1876 eventually became the Saint Walburga home for elderly ladies.

The area surrounding the mansion came to be known as Kaulmont.

Some argue that the formation of the Rescue Hose Company began in 1873 and another in 1874 when the Kaul home burned in 1876.

Newspaper journalists wrote that many more would have been saved were the village to have had a fire company.

Later in August of that year, the newspaper praised the new company for keeping damage at a minimum when fire broke out at Bayer's Furniture Factory and Carpentry School.

It was 1883, thirty years since a handful of settlers spent their first miserable Christmas in Saint Marystown. They were cold, hungry and without religious services.

Saint Marystown was growing up. It had a bank and soon would have its third church. Grist mills, sawmills, dry good shops, and livery stables had been established, many of the colony's sons had fought and died to secure the Union, and there were schools, a band, a fire company, baseball teams, doctors, lawyers, hotels, and a newspaper.

Marienstadt was becoming Saint Marys.

Brother William's Christmas creches (called "cribs") were attracting many admirers to the Saint Marys Church

The railroad had brought real coin of the realm into Saint Marys and with it came the leisure time for the men to utilize their woodworking and toy making skills while their wives baked cakes and cookies.

257

Some of the merchants were even stocking "store boughten" sweetmeats, sleds, wagons, dolls, pop guns, and storybooks.

Church choirs and organs resounded with "Es ist ein Ros Entsprungen, Joseph Lieber Joseph Mein," and other songs and carols which expressed the Angel's timeless message of "Peace Among Men of Good Will."

The town was neither that of law and order nor idyllic. Newspapers reported public drunkenness and brawling when the "hicks" came to town on Saturdays. Shootings and armed robbery were not uncommon. Thus, Saint Marys was in many ways, very much a frontier town.

In 1877, a lady named, Mrs. Bricklemeyer took an axe to her drunken and abusive husband.

He lived and is thought to have changed his ways.

A Mr. Horack was killed in downtown Saint Marys when a "quiet, industrious" citizen threw a rock and hit him in the head. Horack had once served a term for murder, but the rock throwing was unprovoked. The "quiet" and "industrious" perpetrator was acquitted of all charges.

In 1880, a Bennett's Valley badman, while being pursued by a posse, shot and killed constable Frank Warnith of Benzinger Township. He also wounded

another constable, Phillip Volmer.

Harry English, the outlaw, escaped with a bullet in the leg.

Three months later, English was arrested without incident by a Pinkerton agent in Cheboygon, Michigan.

An Elk County jury found English guilty of forgery but exonerated him from Constable Warnith's death. Interestingly, after suffering terribly for eight months as a result of the gunfight, Constable Volmer of Saint Marys also died

For over three decades, **Babylon**, on Cross Road, served as one of the most popular gathering places in the Saint Marys area.

Babylon originated when Joe Dorner put a brewery on the land. Thereafter, Edward Babel acquired the property and bestowed the famous name upon the place.

Although the community often gathered in Babylon, no photos or details of the famous party spot seem to have survived.

The locale was the scene of church picnics, the destination of, Memorial Day parades, 4th of July celebrants, school May walks, and a favorite weekend port of call for many Saint Marys families.

261

Along with the brewery, Dorner and later Babe constructed a large house, baseball fields, a rifle range, a lawn bowling green, dance pavilion and an unmotorized merry-go-round. Special trains running from Saint Marys and Ridgway dropped folk off at the Cross Road crossing near Silver Creek. These would walk up the country road, stopping to examine a large, exposed fossil halfway up the trail.

In 1874, a large group parade with three bands marched from Center Street to Babylon. Also included in the march were one hundred and fifty miners and ten mules.

Following Babel's propriety, Babylon fell upon hard times, and a house of "ill repute" operated there until the citizens demanded that it close.

Finally, in the early 1900s, a large pig farm flourished on the spot, and for the first half of the 20th century, Cross Road was called the Pig Farm Road.

The first fire tower in Saint Marystown was situated on the right side of Lafayette Street in 1873.

In 1873, a large Hall Hardware store opened on North Saint Marys Street. In 1876, it became the Hall & Kaul Department store.

The third floor was named, Olympic Hall, and Jane Eyre was the first play to be performed.

In 1876, the Hardware store became the Hall & Kaul Department store, and in 1924, the old store and the theater became The Boy's Club.

Dr. and Mrs. Eben Russ built their neo-Georgian mansion on Center Street in 1878-79.

In 1921, they donated the house to the community for use as a public library.

In 1878 a stone wall was constructed on the northern bank of the Elk Creek along Depot Street.

Anyone who could get a gun in in the late 1800s often shot passenger pigeons when the vast flocks flew over the town.

Tens of thousands were shot in the Windfall and Rosely section alone.

In 1882, Anthony Auman is said to have killed fourteen with one shot.

Flocks of passenger pigeons would darken the skies for days, filling trees, breaking branches, and defecating on their cousins roosting below. In September 1914, the last known survivor of those unbelievable flocks died in the Cincinnati 200.

Some estimate that there were as many as five billion passenger pigeons in Ohio, Indiana, and Kentucky alone.

Meanwhile, in Elk County a five-foot long Catamount (Puma/Panther/Cougar/Mountain Lion) was killed in the Straight Creek area by Joe Hanes and B. Frank in July 1877.

It was the first recorded big cat kill in fifteen years.

265

It is of interest to note that in 1877, there was an attempt to ban deer hunting in Elk County for five years.

The bill passed the House but was defeated in the Senate.

In the autumn of 1878, a bald eagle was observed soaring over Iron Run and up and down Elk Creek.

The importance of baseball in small town, USA, during the latter half of the 19th century can hardly be overstated.

Before the age of quick and easy entertainment, everyone "went out to the Ballgame."

Thirty years after its founding, Saint Marys had at least four teams, the Modocs, Experts, Sabbaths, and Daisy Cutters. No one was paid to play, and no one paid to watch.

Makeshift baseball fields popped up everywhere: Sugar Hill, Knight's Hill, Bunker Hill, Center Street, Rosely Street, Washington Road, Theresa Road, Cross Road and so on. There were no fences, bleachers, or back stops. Likewise, the players had little or no equipment.

Entertainment in the mid-1800s was not sedentary. Rather, it was participatory and frequently thinly described labor which included barn and house raisings, thrashing/butchering parties, and quilting events.

Apple butter and sauerkraut chopping sessions were popular and commonplace.

Back in the day, most St. Marystown men possessed the ability to play a bit of something on at least one musical instrument.

Between 1860 and 1880, as many as a dozen bands and orchestras were organized, usually with the assistance of Ignatius Garner and/or Professor F. Barnhardt.

On the other end, women were busy having kids, mending socks, making soap, forming candles, churning butter, gathering eggs, scrubbing, cooking, and canning.

In the late 1800s, a never-ending parade of itinerant peddlers and door to door salesmen of every ilk and description made their way over the country byways through the American villages and towns.

These included tinkers, scissor & knife sharpeners, umbrella repairman, bone & rag collectors, patent medicine salesmen, organ grinders, small circus & actor groups, con men of every sort -- and vagrants.

It is likely that there were "traveling men" on the streets every day from April until November from 1855 through 1935. Many of these were unemployed veterans in the post-Civil War years.

Often, these traveling men were the only connection the homebound women and girls had with the world outside of their town, so these also served as de facto newspaper, magazine, and gossip columnists.

Among the transients were homeless men roving the countryside and selling their labor as handymen for bed, bread, and pocket change.

Some hired on for the day, others for weeks, while some married the farmer's daughter and settled down.

Most were likely driven by a relentless wanderlust.

My father, who grew up in the Pilz farmhouse (the original section of the hospital), often spoke of those men, some of whom were always on hire.

A few came close to joining the family.

James Whitcomb Riley's (1849-1916) poetry painted a vivid picture of pre-20th Century rural America.

"W'y, The Raggedy Man—he's ist so good,
He splits the kindlin' an' chops the wood.

An' nen he spades in our garden, too,
An' does most things 'at boys can't do.He clumbed clean up in our big treeAn' shooked a' apple down fer me—An' 'nother 'n', too, fer 'Lizabuth Ann—
An' 'nother 'n', too, fer The Raggedy Man.—

Ain't he a' awful kind Raggedy Man?
Raggedy! Raggedy! Raggedy Man!"

U.S. Grant
1822-1885
Elected 1868-1872

"The Grant Years" (1869-1877) are often considered to have been the most corrupt presidency in American history.

Grant, a famous general and an honest man, had little political talent and surrounded himself with political pirates and opportunists.

During his tenure, Colorado was admitted to the Union, and the transcontinental railroad was completed.

The telephone, barbed wire and the electric light were invented during his years in office.

Much of the fighting in what are called **The Indian Wars** ((1850-1900) occurred during the Grant presidency.

Contrary to the beliefs of many, native Americans were also guilty of many massacrees, and the wars began following the Sioux' attrocities around Fort Laramie, WY, in 1850.

These wars ended when Apache's were finally pacified in 1900.

Granted, the United States Government often acted in bad faith and was also guilty of several slaughters

Whatever-the-case, the Indians were never able to adequately unify.

The best known incidents of the Indian Wars are the battle of Bear Paw Mountain, Tule Lake and the massacres at Wouned Knee and Sand Creek.

The most famous battle is likely Little Big Horn where General George A. Custer pitted 210 cavalrymen carrying single shot breech loaders against three times as many Sioux, many of whom utilized lever action rifes.

Just who or what was to blame for Custer's defeat at the Little Big Horn on June 25, 1876, is not entirely known.

No St. Mary's men are listed as having been veterans of Indian wars, but the late Jim King is said to have been a direct descendent of one of Custer's scouts.

Across the ocean, the great **Queen Victoria** was well into her reign.

In America, the period was known as the Victorian Age and at the time, Great Britain was at the peak of its power with sovereignty over a quarter of the world's surface.

Victoria's greatness derived from her ability to accept the changing role and the competence of the politicians, artists, and visionaries of her time. Among them were Lords Salisbury, Palmerston Disraeli, Gladstone, Dickens, Darwin, Peel, Rhodes, Gilbert & Sullivan, the Bronte's, John Cardinal, Newman, Tennyson, Wilde, Huxley, Spencer, Lister, Elliot, and Wordsworth, et al.

Continental Europe was in the midst of numerous "small" wars, internal revolutions, political assassinations, rampant colonialism, and arbitrary alliances.

An unsuspecting world was setting the stage for the conflagrations of the 20th Century.

273

"THE SUN NEVER SETS ON THE BRITISH EMPIRE"
F.P. DUNNE 1898,
ON VICTORIAN ENGLAND

The Swedish scientist **Alfred's Nobel's** invention of dynamite in 1867 made nitroglycerine safe for mining and construction.

It would also be the building block for destructive weapons.

Other Victorian figures who greatly influenced the creation of modern Europe included **Guiseppa Garibal** and **Otto von Bismark.**

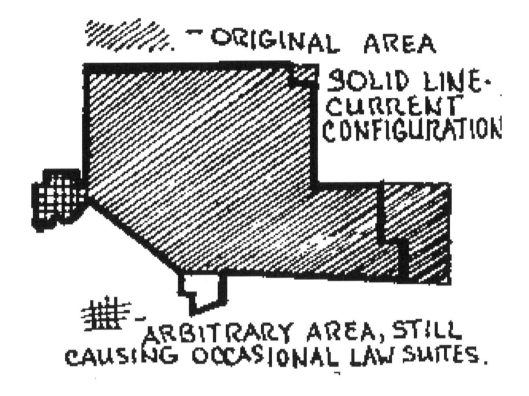

Elk County was created on April 18, 1843, from parts of Jefferson, Clearfield, and McKean Counties. It became the namesake of the elk that roamed the county.

Up to 1873, PA's borders remained in a state of flux. Then, in 1860, Gibson and Shippen Townships on the Eastern side were surrendered to establish Cameron County.

When Millstone was acquired in 1870, an unending dispute began as to just where the Elk/Jefferson ought to have been.

Pennsylvania would continue to evolve until 1873 when the final addition, Lackawanna was chartered.

In the latter half of the 19th century, when many of PA's 67 counties were established, the location of the courthouse (County Seat) was important, for it provided a slight edge to the smaller villages in their potential for survival.

The first court sessions in what is now Elk County were held in Caledonia. Plans to build a courthouse motivated numerous offers of land and money and attempts were made to locate the courthouse in Benezette. However, in 1844, Jacob Ridgway's offer was accepted, and the courthouse was built in Ridgway.

The erection of the house in Ridgway did not end the controversy. **William Stokes** Esq., Philadelphia lawyer and associate of the Benzinger/Eschbach connection, with the assistance of A.I. Wilcox in Harrisburg, attempted but failed to move it to Saint Marys.

1845-1879

Ignatius Garner and the Honorable Charles Luhr worked toward the same end.

A trace of the antagonism seems still to be with us and also seems to have initiated an epidemic in PA, as attempts were made to change the county seats in Jefferson, Clearfield, Warren, and McKean Counties.

Soon after establishing themselves in Saint Marys, the Benedictine Fathers became men on horseback, taking services and sacraments to Catholic settlers as far away as Warren, Smethport, and Brookville.

In some of those villages, Mission churches were built and still serve as parishes today.

After the arrival of the railroads, the range of the Saint Marys Benedictines extended down the Susquehanna and as far as Lock Haven when the area was still attached to Bellefonte.

Ultimately, the missions would fall under the jurisdiction of secular priests from the newly formed Erie Diocese.

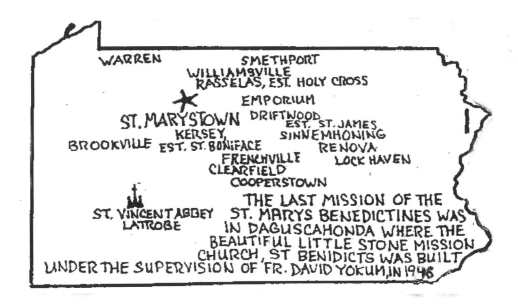

Shortly following the founding of the Saint Joseph Convent in Saint Marys, a group of five nuns set out to establish a foundation in Minnesota which was another of Mother Benedicta and Riepp's visions.

Bishop Josue Young side-tracked the expedition and with Reverend Thomas Mullen convinced the sisters to shelf their cloistered plans and instead become educators in Erie.

Such would the begin an outgrowth of the American motherhouse which would include convents, schools, academies, nurseries, foundations, missions, rest homes, retreat centers, orphanages, homes for the aged, a military academy, all spanning from Kersey to Saint Cloud, Minnesota and from Lucinda to the Isle of Pines, Cuba.

Hundreds of thousands have been educated and cared for both directly and indirectly via the efforts of the "Cradle of the Order" in Saint Marys, PA.

One of the most interesting and informative documents relating to 1870's Elk and Cameron counties is the D.G. Beers & Company map of 1871. It is a subscriber map, so only those stores and businesses which paid a fee are listed. Fortunately, it seems most in business did subscribe.

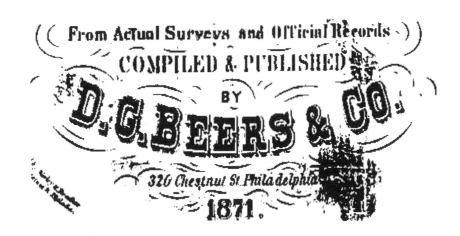

The information available from this old map, a portion of which is copied here, is endless. A quick look shows us that the Diamond was still called the "Common" and Brusselles Street was still named Rosely Street.

The map is hanging for public inspection on the first floor of the Saint Marys Historical Society.

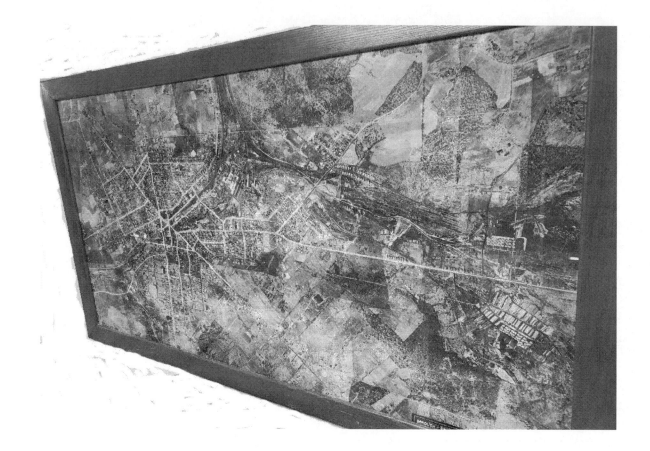

Of the many curious items on the map, perhaps the most interesting is the planned Irish section. Only two dwellings appear on Maurus Street, west of the church.

They were just opposite the Convent entrance, but the property occupied by Elk Catholic High was laid out in lots (about 200) and streets: Shamrock, Rupert, Patrick, Amandus, and Erin.

Today, those street names are long forgotten as are many of the Irish names that were such a prominent segment of the Saint Mary's population in the early railroad years.

There is an apparent lack of documented information regarding the early borough school. It's thought that a small building in the Redemptorist complex served the purpose.

This same building was used as a sheep cote later by the Pilz family when they occupied the premises.

The next borough school of which we know is the brick building that opened on the Maurus/Church Street's corner. In 1875, the sheep cote which stood well into the 1900s would have been the last remnant of the Redemptorist's quarters.

There seems to be more documentation relating to the Township schools albeit much remains unclear. We do know that fifteen years after the colony was founded, a school opened which came to be known as "Windfall."

In 1902, a second floor was added to the school, giving it two rooms. During the "dry" years, the building served as a speakeasy and later, the Windfall Inn. No alarm sounded when it burned under mysterious circumstances in 1934.

County school records suggest that there were fifty-five one-room schoolhouses in the Saint Marys/Benzinger area in the late 1800s.

The crudest of these seems to have been the tiny Log "Weigel" school on the corner of Alphonse (Ford) and the present-day South Saint Marys Road.

The young township teachers, derived mostly from two-year state normal programs, were often no older than their eldest students.

Romance and Marriage were not uncommon.

Because teachers from the State Normal Schools were often young and female, turnover was frequent. School districts and boards attempted to attend to the issue with a series of laws and rules, some of which included:

- You will not marry during contract term.
- You may not keep company with men.
- You must be in between 8 p.m. and 6 p.m.
- You may not loiter in ice cream stores.
- You must have the Board's permission to travel outside the township.
- You may not dress in bright colors.
- You must start a fire every morning by 7:00 a.m. so the room is warm by 8:00 a.m.

However, it was no easier to legislate romance then than it is today, and many of the young teachers roomed at the farmhouses near the school. Such houses were often the homes of young men of marriageable age.

There are reasons to believe that in the early colony years, no distinction was made between town and country, and most of the children, no matter where they lived, learned the three Rs from the priests, nuns, and brothers.

Township School No. 1 stood on the site of the present-day Post Office. It moved at least twice - most Township schools often did - and added a number of rooms. It is also thought to have been referred to as "The Central School."

One of the first township owned buildings stood near the Depot Street parking lot but was seldom, if ever, used as a schoolhouse, having been located too far away from the Convent.

The building assumed the role as railroad tool shed and telegraph office in 1890.

The Saint Joseph Convent Sisters taught in the Saint Benedict Academy, the Saint Marys Borough School. Two of the four teachers at the Township High School on Chestnut were Benedictine nuns.

There were a few male teachers in the 19th century schoolhouses; but, as one might expect, they do not seem to have been restricted by repressive rules.

One-room schoolhouses were rarely "one room" or even a single story.

Notwithstanding Windfall, the Saint Marys Street School and the South Michael Road schools were two-storied.

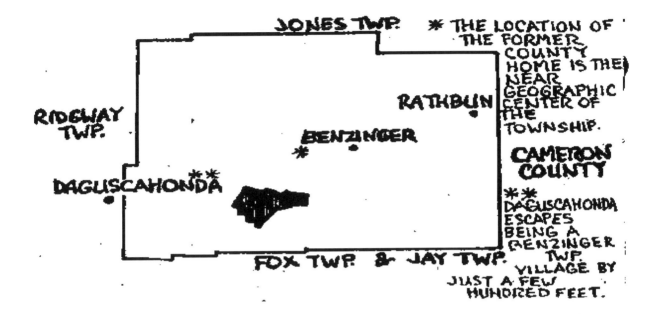

Saint Marys and its formerly surrounding Township in many ways constitute a unique and curious symbiosis.

The original Redemptorist idea, which would have given each settler a town and country lot, meant that everyone living in Saint Marys would have been a citizen of both village and surrounding township.

For years, the village and township schools comprised a single system. Likewise, the mail sent to Saint Marys was addressed to the "Benzinger" Post Office until well into the 1870s.

Unlike the other Elk County Townships, Benzinger had but one community within its boundaries.

Its two largest settlements, Rathbun and Benzinger were pieces of Saint Marys, Lynchville, and Kaulmont.

Interestingly, the waters of the West Creek on the eastern side of the Township are the headwaters of the Sinnemahoning and flow into the Chesapeake Bay.

285

Silver Creek, Ten Cent Run, Iron Run and Laurel Run flow into the Elk Creek, the Clarion, the Allegheny, the Ohio, Mississippi, and ultimately in the Gulf of Mexico.

In the early years, the line between Town and Township signified little. The planned center of the town was not even in the Borough, as there was little political activity prior to 1933 when a group formed a taxpayer's league.

The early additions were made to include expanding industry. The curious indentation went around the Kaul home.

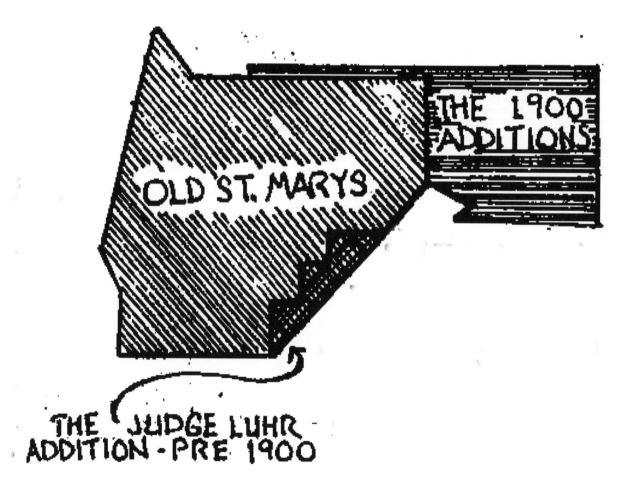

Work, prior to the industrial revolution, was temporary and seasonal. Warm winter shut down logging camps and prevented harvested wood from being marketed.

A poor growing season would mean crop failure, and the men who worked as harvest-time farm hands were deprived of their source of income.

In the late 1800's, there was neither workman's compensation nor unemployment pay.

Ice harvesting was great importance.

A winter without ice was a disaster, as enough had to be cut to last until the next yearly freeze.

Some of the ice ponds were located at the Convent, upper Center Street, and along the Elk Creek and North Saint Marys Road. The cutting tools were local products.

Wild berry picking was another seasonal occupation. The homemade metal backpack buckets are thought to have been unique to the area.

Many pickers wore old socks on their hands.

Strawberries, Juneberries, teaberries, choke cherries, huckleberries, raspberries, dewberries, elderberries, and cranberries were all harvested. These were used for baking, preserves, and sometimes added to catsups, tonics, sauces, wines, and cordials.

"Sugaring" entailed the extraction of sugar and syrup from maple trees. It was an intense process and yielded a low volume. Little was as dependent on the weather as sugaring.

Freezing nights above 20 degrees were necessary as well as thawing days with temperatures in the high 30s. It was a precarious business.

One aspect of life in the *Good Old Days* often overlooked by today's standards is that 19th century America did not smell good. In fact, few of us today would happily tolerate such a rich, "heady" atmosphere.

Much of the homemade soaps used during the period were made from lime, wood ash, and kitchen grease. Hot washing water was heated on the stove and often used by more than one family member. Few bathed more than once a week.

The odor of kerosene lamps, wood stoves, and coal furnaces floated in the air, a steady string of locomotives belched soot, while the sour smell of curing wood and the fragrance of animal hides emanated from sawmills and tanneries.

Adding to the stench of the atmosphere was the effluvium rising from the waterways.

Hair, clothing, and furniture absorbed the ambrosia.

Decades of horse manure ground into the roads reeked after a summer rain.

Cows roamed free on the streets, and herds of cattle were driven though the town on their way to stockyards and slaughterhouses on Center and North Saint Marys Street.

No matter how elegantly adorned, one's odor exemplified ample evidence of livestock residue.

There was little indoor plumbing, and the privy or "necessary" played an important role in every home, both in town and in the countryside.

"Honey Dippers" or "Night-Soil-Gatherers" maintained the privies and were a constant and necessary presence on the street.

The latter half of the 19th century was not a time for faint hearts or delicate nostrils.

During the late 1860s, the Kaul business ventures grew ever more varied. By 1873, Andrew Kaul had extended his timbering operations into the Sterling Run area of Cameron County.

J.K.P. Hall

(1844-1915)

PA State Senate
U.S. Congress

In 1871, he entered into a partnership with J.K.P. Hall, and many businesses developed as a result.

The chemistry between the two men was nearly perfect, and their vision and entrepreneurship were major factors in the growth of El County and the Saint Marys area.

Shortly after the Hall-Kaul affiliation, they purchased pine stands in Wisconsin. Sales of those lands allowed for further acquisitions of large tracts in Elk and Cameron Counties.

In 1879, Kaul, with his partner, Hall, moved into the growing coal business.

Their Cascade, the Hazel Dell, and Keystone mines, were located in the eastern section of Saint Marys in the Brusselles, Rosely, Eschbach area.

In 1880, one hundred-thirty men averaged two tons of coal per worker every day in the Cascade hole.

The partnership of Andrew Kaul and Jim Hall resulted in Kaul's affiliation with Hall's Saint Marys Bank. The institution would evolve into the Saint Marys National Bank and the Saint Marys Trust Company.

They extended their logging and mining enterprises to Clermont, Byrndale, Cardiff, Paine, and Kersey.

The railroads they built to serve those operations would serve as the foundation of the PS&N Railway System and Shawmut Mining Company.

End of Part one...

Index of Names

About the Author

Richard (Dick) Dornisch was the husband of Mary and the father of Hugh, Blaise, Claude, Joel, and Denise.

He was a veteran of the U.S. Army Signal Corps, local politician, author, and journalist.

He was also an artist, literary critic, naturalist, Christmas hobbyist, and photojournalist, who loved folklore, politics, military tradition, aviation, bird watching, hunting wildflowers, and molding lead soldiers.

Dick formed a Book Club in 1956 which 50 years later had read upwards of 900 books.

The Book Club continues to meet at the time of this publication.

Aside from Dick's many interests, he also enjoyed gathering with friends and served as St. Marystown's evening provocateur at various restaurants and other establishments.

Made in the USA
Middletown, DE
14 August 2021